PRENTICE HALL
SCIENCE EXPLORER

Weather and Climate

Prentice
Hall

Needham, Massachusetts
Upper Saddle River, New Jersey
Glenview, Illinois

Weather and Climate

Book-Specific Resources

Student Edition
Annotated Teacher's Edition
Teaching Resources with Color Transparencies
Consumable and Nonconsumable Materials Kits
Guided Reading Audio CDs
Guided Reading Audiotapes
Guided Reading and Study Workbook
Guided Reading and Study Workbook, Teacher's Edition
Lab Activity Videotapes
Science Explorer Videotapes
Science Explorer Web Site at **www.phschool.com**

Program-Wide Resources

Computer Test Bank Book with CD-ROM
How to Assess Student Work
How to Manage Instruction in the Block
Inquiry Skills Activity Book
Integrated Science Laboratory Manual
Integrated Science Laboratory Manual, Teacher's Edition
Interactive Student Tutorial CD-ROM
Prentice Hall Interdisciplinary Explorations
Probeware Lab Manual
Product Testing Activities by Consumer Reports™
Program Planning Guide
Reading in the Content Area with Literature Connections
Resource Pro® CD-ROM (Teaching Resources on CD-ROM)
Science Explorer Videodiscs
Standardized Test Preparation Book
Student-Centered Science Activity Books
Teacher's ELL Handbook: Strategies for English Language Learners

Spanish Resources

Spanish Student Edition
Spanish Guided Reading Audio CDs with Section Summaries
Spanish Guided Reading Audiotapes with Section Summaries
Spanish Science Explorer Videotapes

Science Explorer Student Editions

From Bacteria to Plants

Animals

Cells and Heredity

Human Biology and Health

Environmental Science

Inside Earth

Earth's Changing Surface

Earth's Waters

Weather and Climate

Astronomy

Chemical Building Blocks

Chemical Interactions

Motion, Forces, and Energy

Electricity and Magnetism

Sound and Light

Acknowledgments

Acknowledgment for pages 150-151: Excerpt from *Alone* by Richard E. Byrd. Copyright ©1938 by Richard E. Byrd. Reprinted by permission of Island Press.

ISBN 0-13-054085-4
2 3 4 5 6 7 8 9 10   04 03 02

Cover: Lightning flashes over Tucson, Arizona.

Program Authors

Michael J. Padilla, Ph.D.
Professor
Department of Science Education
University of Georgia
Athens, Georgia

Michael Padilla is a leader in middle school science education. He has served as an editor and elected officer for the National Science Teachers Association. He has been principal investigator of several National Science Foundation and Eisenhower grants and served as a writer of the National Science Education Standards.

As lead author of *Science Explorer,* Mike has inspired the team in developing a program that meets the needs of middle grades students, promotes science inquiry, and is aligned with the National Science Education Standards.

Ioannis Miaoulis, Ph.D.
Dean of Engineering
College of Engineering
Tufts University
Medford, Massachusetts

Martha Cyr, Ph.D.
Director, Engineering
  Educational Outreach
College of Engineering
Tufts University
Medford, Massachusetts

Science Explorer was created in collaboration with the College of Engineering at Tufts University. Tufts has an extensive engineering outreach program that uses engineering design and construction to excite and motivate students and teachers in science and technology education.

Faculty from Tufts University participated in the development of *Science Explorer* chapter projects, reviewed the student books for content accuracy, and helped coordinate field testing.

Book Author

Barbara Brooks Simons
Science Writer
Boston, Massachusetts

Contributing Writers

Alfred B. Bortz, Ph.D.
School of Education
Duquesne University
Pittsburgh, Pennsylvania

Emery Pineo
Science Teacher
Barrington Middle School
Barrington, Rhode Island

Karen Riley Sievers
Science Teacher
Callanan Middle School
Des Moines, Iowa

Sharon M. Stroud
Science Teacher
Widefield High School
Colorado Springs, Colorado

Reading Consultant

Bonnie B. Armbruster, Ph.D.
Department of Curriculum
  and Instruction
University of Illinois
Champaign, Illinois

Interdisciplinary Consultant

Heidi Hayes Jacobs, Ed.D.
Teacher's College
Columbia University
New York, New York

Safety Consultants

W. H. Breazeale, Ph.D.
Department of Chemistry
College of Charleston
Charleston, South Carolina

Ruth Hathaway, Ph.D.
Hathaway Consulting
Cape Girardeau, Missouri

Tufts University Program Reviewers

Content Reviewers

Teacher Reviewers

Stephanie Anderson
Sierra Vista Junior
    High School
Canyon Country, California

John W. Anson
Mesa Intermediate School
Palmdale, California

Pamela Arline
Lake Taylor Middle School
Norfolk, Virginia

Lynn Beason
College Station Jr. High School
College Station, Texas

Richard Bothmer
Hollis School District
Hollis, New Hampshire

Jeffrey C. Callister
Newburgh Free Academy
Newburgh, New York

Judy D'Albert
Harvard Day School
Corona Del Mar, California

Betty Scott Dean
Guilford County Schools
McLeansville, North Carolina

Sarah C. Duff
Baltimore City Public Schools
Baltimore, Maryland

Melody Law Ewey
Holmes Junior High School
Davis, California

Sherry L. Fisher
Lake Zurich Middle
    School North
Lake Zurich, Illinois

Melissa Gibbons
Fort Worth ISD
Fort Worth, Texas

Debra J. Goodding
Kraemer Middle School
Placentia, California

Jack Grande
Weber Middle School
Port Washington, New York

Steve Hills
Riverside Middle School
Grand Rapids, Michigan

Carol Ann Lionello
Kraemer Middle School
Placentia, California

Jaime A. Morales
Henry T. Gage Middle School
Huntington Park, California

Patsy Partin
Cameron Middle School
Nashville, Tennessee

Deedra H. Robinson
Newport News Public Schools
Newport News, Virginia

Bonnie Scott
Clack Middle School
Abilene, Texas

Charles M. Sears
Belzer Middle School
Indianapolis, Indiana

Barbara M. Strange
Ferndale Middle School
High Point, North Carolina

Jackie Louise Ulfig
Ford Middle School
Allen, Texas

Kathy Usina
Belzer Middle School
Indianapolis, Indiana

Heidi M. von Oetinger
L'Anse Creuse Public School
Harrison Township, Michigan

Pam Watson
Hill Country Middle School
Austin, Texas

Activity Field Testers

Nicki Bibbo
Russell Street School
Littleton, Massachusetts

Connie Boone
Fletcher Middle School
Jacksonville Beach, Florida

Rose-Marie Botting
Broward County
    School District
Fort Lauderdale, Florida

Colleen Campos
Laredo Middle School
Aurora, Colorado

Elizabeth Chait
W. L. Chenery Middle School
Belmont, Massachusetts

Holly Estes
Hale Middle School
Stow, Massachusetts

Laura Hapgood
Plymouth Community
    Intermediate School
Plymouth, Massachusetts

Sandra M. Harris
Winman Junior High School
Warwick, Rhode Island

Jason Ho
Walter Reed Middle School
Los Angeles, California

Joanne Jackson
Winman Junior High School
Warwick, Rhode Island

Mary F. Lavin
Plymouth Community
    Intermediate School
Plymouth, Massachusetts

James MacNeil, Ph.D.
Concord Public Schools
Concord, Massachusetts

Lauren Magruder
St. Michael's Country
    Day School
Newport, Rhode Island

Jeanne Maurand
Glen Urquhart School
Beverly Farms, Massachusetts

Warren Phillips
Plymouth Community
    Intermediate School
Plymouth, Massachusetts

Carol Pirtle
Hale Middle School
Stow, Massachusetts

Kathleen M. Poe
Kirby-Smith Middle School
Jacksonville, Florida

Cynthia B. Pope
Ruffner Middle School
Norfolk, Virginia

Anne Scammell
Geneva Middle School
Geneva, New York

Karen Riley Sievers
Callanan Middle School
Des Moines, Iowa

David M. Smith
Howard A. Eyer Middle School
Macungie, Pennsylvania

Derek Strohschneider
Plymouth Community
    Intermediate School
Plymouth, Massachusetts

Sallie Teames
Rosemont Middle School
Fort Worth, Texas

Gene Vitale
Parkland Middle School
McHenry, Illinois

Zenovia Young
Meyer Levin Junior
    High School (IS 285)
Brooklyn, New York

Weather and Climate

Activities

Eyes On EARTH

At the Kennedy Space Center on the east coast of Florida, a crew prepares to launch a satellite into space. They know that a thunderstorm may be moving toward them. Should they launch the mission or delay? Before deciding, the crew contacts meteorologists for the latest weather forecast.

The Kennedy Space Center is about 100 kilometers east of the center of the state. More summer thunderstorms occur in central Florida than nearly any other area in the world. Predicting when severe storms will develop and where they will move is one of the most demanding jobs for a meteorologist. One of the best people at this job is J. Marshall Shepherd.

J. Marshall Shepherd
The son of two school principals, J. Marshall Shepherd was born in 1969 and raised in the small town of Canton, Georgia. Today he works for NASA as a research meteorologist for Mission to Planet Earth. He's an expert on the development of powerful thunderstorms. He studied meteorology at Florida State University.

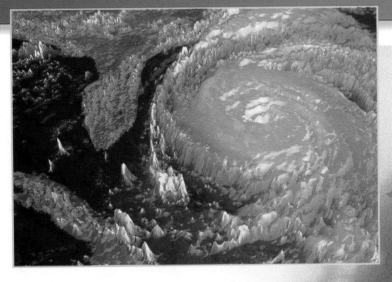

Getting Started at a Science Fair

Marshall Shepherd is an "old hand" at predicting the weather. He's been at it since sixth grade, when his teacher suggested that he enter a science fair. Marshall titled his science project "Can a Sixth-Grader Predict the Weather?" First he toured the local TV station in Atlanta to see what instruments meteorologists use to measure basic weather variables.

> " The shape of Florida is part of the reason that so many storms form here. "

"Then I did a little background reading and decided I could build some of those instruments out of basic materials around the house," he recalls.

Using household materials and a few inexpensive items at supply stores, Marshall Shepherd built everything he needed for his project. He constructed a weather station with an anemometer to measure wind speed, a wind vane to measure wind direction, a barometer to measure air pressure, a hair hygrometer to measure humidity, and a rain gauge.

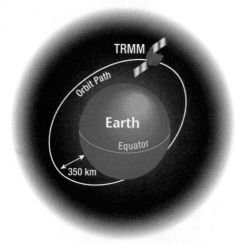

▲ TRMM, a device that records weather conditions from space, orbits Earth at an altitude of 350 kilometers. It flies over each position on Earth at a different time each day.

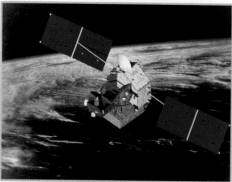

TRMM observatory is about the size of a small room and weighs as much as a medium-sized truck. It contains two solar panels and instruments to record weather data.

"From these basic instruments, I took weather observations around my neighborhood," he explains. "I developed a model of day-to-day weather over a six-month period and found some very interesting and accurate results." Marshall's instruments and scientific work on this project won prizes for him at local, district, and state science fairs.

"From that point on, I was involved with science projects," he recalls. By the time he graduated from high school, he had a definite goal. "One day, I planned to be a research scientist at NASA (National Aeronautics and Space Administration)," he stated.

Predicting Severe Storms

Hurricane Andrew—the most powerful hurricane ever to strike Florida—swept through Southern Florida and Louisiana in 1992. Marshall was in college at the time. "My college research paper was on hurricane tracking using radar. I actually did some work with Hurricane Andrew," he says. "That's how I got interested in tropical weather."

In graduate school, Marshall Shepherd investigated the way powerful thunderstorms form and move, especially those in central Florida. The long, narrow shape of Florida is part of the reason that so many storms form there. "When you have land heating faster than water, you get something called sea-breeze circulation," he explains. "On a typical summer day, a sea-breeze forms on both the west coast and the east coast of Florida. They tend to move toward the center. When they collide, you get intense thunderstorm development."

Designing New Instruments

Now Marshall Shepherd works at NASA, where his projects contribute to NASA's Mission to Planet Earth.

This map was generated by TRMM. The white rectangle identifies a cyclone.

This long-term program uses information from satellites, aircraft, and ground studies to explore environmental changes around the world.

Marshall Shepherd's knowledge of thunderstorms is especially valuable in interpreting data from TRMM (Tropical Rainfall Measuring Mission), a device that measures tropical and subtropical rainfall. Rainfall cycles in tropical regions affect weather throughout the world.

Marshall Shepherd's work involves both observation and calculation. As he did in sixth grade, he designs and builds instruments. But now his devices are some of the most advanced in the world. He no longer takes his instruments into a neighborhood to measure weather conditions directly. Instead, his specialty is "remote sensing"—making observations of weather conditions (rainfall, water vapor, and so on) from a distance.

After collecting data, Marshall uses a computer to analyze it. He and others have designed a computer program that uses the data to predict the development of severe storms. So

when a crew at the Kennedy Space Center must decide whether or not to launch a rocket, they rely on predictions from programs similar to ones that Marshall Shepherd has worked on.

Looking Ahead

Marshall Shepherd's personal goals go beyond Mission to Planet Earth. "With the upcoming international space station, scientists are going to have the opportunity to do research from space. My goal is to conduct Earth-directed meteorological research from the space station as well as from the ground. I'll use some of the new instruments we are currently developing." He describes another important goal back home on Earth—"to reach out, inspire, and expose students to science."

In Your Journal

Marshall Shepherd credits his success to having detailed goals. "I always write down goals, and check them off as they happen," he says. Think of an important task that you would like to accomplish over the next year. Identify the steps and note target dates you will need to meet in order to reach your goal. How do those steps help bring you closer to achieving your goal?

CHAPTER
1 The Atmosphere

WEB ACTIVITY
www.phschool.com

Integrating Environmental Science

Watching the Weather

The air is cool and clear—just perfect for a trip in a hot-air balloon. As you rise, a fresh breeze begins to move you along. Where will it take you? Hot-air balloon pilots need to know about the weather to plot their course.

In this chapter, you will learn about the air around you. As you learn about the atmosphere, you will use your senses to collect information about weather conditions. Even without scientific instruments it is possible to make many accurate observations about the weather.

Your Goal To observe weather conditions without using instruments and to look for hints about tomorrow's weather in the weather conditions today.

Your completed project must
- ◆ include a plan for observing and describing a variety of weather conditions over a period of two to three weeks
- ◆ show your observations in a daily weather log
- ◆ display your findings about weather conditions

Get Started Begin by discussing what weather conditions you can observe. Brainstorm how to use your senses to describe the weather. For example, can you describe the wind speed by observing the school flag? Can you describe the temperature based on what clothes you need to wear outside? Be creative.

Check Your Progress You'll be working on this project as you study this chapter. To keep your project on track, look for Check Your Progress boxes at the following points.

Section 1 Review, page 17: Collect and record observations.
Section 4 Review, page 36: Look for patterns in your data.

Wrap Up At the end of the chapter (page 39), use your weather observations to prepare a display for the class.

Hot-air balloons soar into the atmosphere at a balloon festival in Snowmass, Colorado.

SECTION 1 The Air Around You

DISCOVER .... ACTIVITY

How Long Will the Candle Burn?

1. Put on your goggles.

2. 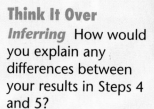 Stick a small piece of modeling clay onto an aluminum pie pan. Push a short candle into the clay. Carefully light the candle.

3. Hold a small glass jar by the bottom. Lower the mouth of the jar over the candle until the jar rests on the pie pan. As you do this, start a stopwatch or note where the second hand is on a clock.

4. Watch the candle carefully. How long does the flame burn?

5. Wearing an oven mitt, remove the jar. Relight the candle and then repeat Steps 3 and 4 with a larger jar.

Think It Over

Inferring How would you explain any differences between your results in Steps 4 and 5?

GUIDE FOR READING

◆ How is the atmosphere important to living things?

◆ What gases are present in Earth's atmosphere?

Reading Tip Before you read, preview Figure 2. As you read, write a sentence about each of the major gases in the atmosphere.

As you walk home from school, the air is warm and still. The sky is full of thick, dark clouds. In the distance you see a bright flash. A few seconds later, you hear a crack of thunder. As you turn the corner onto your street, raindrops start to fall. You begin to run and reach your home just as the downpour begins. That was close! From the shelter of the entrance you pause to catch your breath and watch the storm.

Importance of the Atmosphere

Does the weather where you live change frequently, or is it fairly constant from day to day? **Weather** is the condition of Earth's atmosphere at a particular time and place. But what is the atmosphere? Earth's **atmosphere** (AT muh sfeer) is the layer of gases that surrounds the planet. To understand the relative size of the atmosphere, imagine that the planet Earth is the size of an apple.

Figure 1 When seen from space, Earth's atmosphere appears as a thin layer near the horizon. The atmosphere makes life on Earth possible.

14 ◆ 1

If you breathe on the apple, a thin film of water will form on its surface. Earth's atmosphere is like that water on the apple—a thin layer of gases on Earth's surface.

Earth's atmosphere makes conditions on Earth suitable for living things. The atmosphere contains oxygen and other gases that you and other living things need to live. In turn, living things affect the atmosphere. The atmosphere is constantly changing, with atoms and molecules of gases moving around the globe and in and out of living things, the land, and the water.

Living things also need warmth and liquid water. By trapping energy from the sun, the atmosphere keeps most of Earth's surface warm enough for water to exist as a liquid. In addition, Earth's atmosphere protects living things from dangerous radiation from the sun. It also prevents Earth's surface from being hit by most meteoroids, or chunks of rock from outer space.

☑ *Checkpoint* *What would conditions on Earth be like without the atmosphere?*

Composition of the Atmosphere

The atmosphere is made up of a mixture of atoms and molecules of different kinds of gases. An atom is the smallest unit of a chemical element that can exist by itself. Molecules are made up of two or more atoms. **Earth's atmosphere is made up of nitrogen, oxygen, carbon dioxide, water vapor, and many other gases, as well as particles of liquids and solids.**

Nitrogen As you can see in Figure 2, nitrogen is the most abundant gas in the atmosphere. It makes up a little more than three fourths of the air we breathe. Each nitrogen molecule consists of two nitrogen atoms.

Language Arts
CONNECTION

The word *atmosphere* comes from two Greek words: *atmos*, meaning "vapor," and *sphaira*, meaning "ball," or "globe." So the atmosphere is the vapors or gases surrounding a globe—in this case, Earth.

In Your Journal

As you read this chapter, write down all the words that end in *-sphere*. Look up the roots of each word in a dictionary. How does knowing the roots of each word help you understand its meaning?

Gases in Dry Air

Nitrogen (78%)
Oxygen (21%)
All other gases (1%)

Other Gases	Percentage by Volume
Argon	0.93
Carbon dioxide	0.036
Neon	0.0018
Helium	0.00052
Methane	0.00015
Krypton	0.00011
Hydrogen	0.00005

Figure 2 Dry air in the lower atmosphere always has the same composition of gases. *Interpreting Data What two gases make up most of the air?*

Breathe In, Breathe Out

How can you detect carbon dioxide in the air you exhale?

1. Put on your goggles.
2. Fill a glass or beaker halfway with limewater.

3. Using a straw, slowly blow air through the limewater for about a minute. **CAUTION:** *Do not suck on the straw or drink the limewater.*
4. What happens to the limewater?

Developing Hypotheses What do you think would happen if you did the same experiment after jogging for 10 minutes? If you tried this, what might the results tell you about exercise and carbon dioxide?

INTEGRATING
LIFE SCIENCE

Nitrogen is essential to living things. Proteins and other complex chemical substances in living things contain nitrogen. You and all other organisms must have nitrogen in order to grow and to repair body cells.

Most living things cannot obtain nitrogen directly from the air. Instead, some bacteria convert nitrogen into substances called nitrates. Plants then absorb the nitrates from the soil and use them to make proteins. To obtain proteins, animals must eat plants or other animals.

Oxygen Most oxygen molecules have two oxygen atoms. Even though oxygen is the second-most abundant gas in the atmosphere, it makes up less than one fourth of the volume. Plants and animals take oxygen directly from the air and use it to release energy from food in a usable form.

Oxygen is also involved in other important processes. Any fuel you can think of, from the gasoline in a car to the candles on a birthday cake, uses oxygen as it burns. Without oxygen, a fire will go out. Burning uses oxygen rapidly. During other processes, oxygen is used slowly. For example, steel in cars and other objects reacts slowly with oxygen to form iron oxide, or rust.

Have you ever noticed a pungent smell in the air after a thunderstorm? This is the odor of ozone, which forms when lightning interacts with oxygen in the air. **Ozone** is a form of oxygen that has three oxygen atoms in each molecule instead of the usual two.

Carbon Dioxide Each molecule of carbon dioxide has one atom of carbon and two atoms of oxygen. Even though the atmosphere contains only a small amount of carbon dioxide, it is essential to life. Plants must have carbon dioxide to produce food. Animals, on the other hand, give off carbon dioxide as a waste product.

When fuels such as coal and gasoline are burned, they release carbon dioxide. Burning these fuels increases the amount of carbon dioxide in the atmosphere. Rising carbon dioxide levels may be raising Earth's temperature. The issue of Earth's rising temperature, or global warming, is discussed in Chapter 4.

Figure 3 To burn, these candles need oxygen, one of the gases in the atmosphere. *Predicting What would happen if the candles used up all of the oxygen around them?*

Other Gases Oxygen and nitrogen together make up 99 percent of dry air. Carbon dioxide and argon make up most of the other one percent. The remaining gases are called trace gases because only small amounts of them are present.

Water Vapor The composition of the air discussed so far has been for dry air. In reality, air is not dry because it contains water vapor. **Water vapor** is water in the form of a gas. Water vapor is invisible—it is not the same thing as steam, which is made up of tiny droplets of liquid water. Each water molecule contains two atoms of hydrogen and one atom of oxygen.

The amount of water vapor in the air varies greatly from place to place and from time to time. Air above a desert or polar ice sheet may contain almost no water vapor. In tropical rain forests, on the other hand, as much as five percent of the air may be water vapor.

Water vapor plays an important role in Earth's weather. Clouds form when water vapor condenses out of the air to form tiny droplets of liquid water or crystals of ice. If these droplets or crystals become large enough, they can fall as rain or snow.

Particles Pure air contains only gases. But pure air exists only in laboratories. In the real world, air also contains tiny solid and liquid particles of dust, smoke, salt, and other chemicals. Sometimes you can see particles in the air around you, but most of them are too small to see.

Figure 4 This lush vegetation grows in a rain forest in Costa Rica. The percentage of water vapor in the air in a rain forest may be as high as five percent.

Section 1 Review

1. Describe two ways in which the atmosphere is important to life on Earth.
2. What are the four most common gases in dry air?
3. Why are the amounts of gases in the atmosphere usually shown as percentages of dry air?
4. **Thinking Critically** **Applying Concepts** How would the amount of carbon dioxide in the atmosphere change if there were no plants? If there were no animals?

Check Your Progress
Have you determined *how*, *where*, and *when*, you will make your observations? Organize a notebook to record them. Think of ways to compare weather conditions from day to day. Make your observations without weather instruments or TV weather reports. (*Hint:* You can estimate how much of the sky is covered by clouds.) For your own safety, do not try to make observations during storms.

CHAPTER PROJECT 1

How Clean Is the Air?

Sometimes you can actually see the atmosphere! How? Since air is normally transparent, it can only be visible because it contains particles. In this activity, you will use a vacuum cleaner to gather particles from the air.

Problem

How do weather factors affect the number of particles in the air?

Skills Focus

measuring, interpreting data

Materials

coffee filters
rubber band
thermometer
low-power microscope
vacuum cleaner with intake hose (1 per class)

Procedure

1. Predict what factors will affect the number of particles you collect. How might different weather factors affect your results?
2. In your notebook, make a data table like the one below.
3. Place the coffee filter over the nozzle of the vacuum cleaner hose. Fasten the coffee filter securely to the hose with a rubber band. Make sure the air passes through the coffee filter before entering the vacuum cleaner.
4. You will take air samples in the same place each day for five days. If possible, find a place outdoors. Otherwise, you can run the vacuum cleaner out a classroom window. **CAUTION:** *Do not use the vacuum cleaner outdoors on wet or rainy days.* If it is wet or rainy, collect the sample as soon as possible after it stops raining.
5. Hold the vacuum nozzle at least one meter above the ground each time you use the vacuum. Turn on the vacuum. Run the vacuum for 30 minutes. Shut off the vacuum.

DATA TABLE					
Date and Time	Temperature	Amount of Precipitation	Wind Direction	Wind Speed	Number of Particles

6. While the vacuum is running, observe the weather conditions. Measure the temperature. Estimate the amount of precipitation, if any, since the previous observation. Note the direction from which the wind, if any, is blowing. Also note whether the wind is heavy, light, or calm. Record your observations.

7. Remove the coffee filter from the nozzle. Label the filter with the place, time, and date. Draw a circle on the filter to show the area that was over the vacuum nozzle.

8. Place the coffee filter on the stage of a microscope (40 power). Be sure that the part of the filter that was over the vacuum nozzle is directly under the microscope lens. Without moving the coffee filter, count all the particles you see. Record the number in your data table.

9. Repeat Steps 3–8 each clear day.

Analyze and Conclude

1. Was there a day of the week when you collected more particles?

2. What factors changed during the week that could have caused changes in the particle count?

3. Did the weather have any effect on your day-to-day results? If so, which weather factor do you think was most important?

4. Make a list of some possible sources of the particles you collected. Are these sources natural, or did the particles come from manufactured products?

5. How could you improve your method to get more particles out of the air?

6. **Apply** Identify areas in or around your school where there may be high levels of dust and other particles. What can people do to protect themselves in these areas?

Design an Experiment

Do you think time of day will affect the number of particles you collect? Develop a hypothesis and a plan for testing it. Could you work with other classes to get data at different times of the day? Before carrying out your plan, get your teacher's approval.

INTEGRATING ENVIRONMENTAL SCIENCE

SECTION 2 Air Quality

DISCOVER — ACTIVITY

What's On the Jar?

1. Put on your goggles.
2. Put a small piece of modeling clay on a piece of aluminum foil. Push a candle into the clay. Light the candle.
3. Wearing an oven mitt, hold a glass jar by the rim so that the bottom of the jar is just above the flame.

Think It Over

Observing What do you see on the jar? Where did it come from?

GUIDE FOR READING

◆ What are the main sources of air pollution?

◆ How do photochemical smog and acid rain form?

Reading Tip As you read, look for evidence to support this statement: Most air pollution is caused by human activities. What facts support this statement? What facts do not support it?

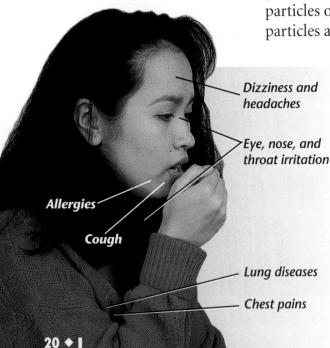

Dizziness and headaches

Eye, nose, and throat irritation

Allergies

Cough

Lung diseases

Chest pains

One hundred years ago, the city of London, England, was dark and dirty. Factories burned coal, and most houses were heated by coal. The air was full of soot. In 1905, the term *smog* was created by combining the words *smoke* and *fog* to describe this type of air pollution. Today, people in London burn much less coal. As a result, the air in London now is much cleaner than it was 100 years ago.

Air Pollution

As you are reading this, you are breathing without even thinking about it. Breathing brings air into your lungs, where the oxygen you need is taken into your body. You may also breathe in tiny particles or even a small amount of harmful gases. In fact, these particles and gases are a concern to people everywhere.

If you live in a large city, you probably already know what air pollution is. You may have noticed a brown haze or an unpleasant smell in the air. Even if you live far from a city, the air around you may be polluted. Harmful substances in the air, water, or soil are known as **pollutants**. Figure 5 shows some of the effects of air pollution on human health.

Figure 5 Air pollution can cause many different problems. Some air pollutants are natural, but most are caused by human activities. *Interpreting Photographs* What parts of the body are most affected by air pollution?

20 ◆ I

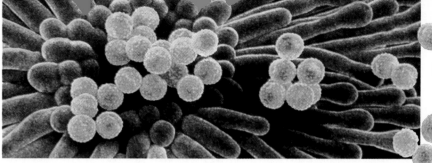

Figure 6 These pollen grains from a ragweed flower have been greatly magnified to show detail. Pollen can cause people who are allergic to it to sneeze.

Some air pollution occurs naturally, but much of it is caused by human activities. **Most air pollution is the result of burning fossil fuels such as coal, oil, gasoline, and diesel fuel.** Almost half of the air pollution from human activities comes from cars and other motor vehicles. A little more than one fourth comes from factories and power plants that burn coal and oil. Burning fossil fuels produces a number of air pollutants, including particles and gases that can form smog and acid rain.

☑ *Checkpoint* *What are two sources of air pollution that you see every day?*

Particles

As you know, air contains particles along with gases. When you draw these particles deep into your lungs, the particles can be harmful. Particles in the air come from both natural sources and human activities.

Natural Sources Many natural processes add particles to the atmosphere. When ocean waves splash salt water against rocks, some of the water sprays into the air and evaporates. Tiny salt particles stay in the air. The wind blows particles of molds and plant pollen. Forest fires, soil erosion, and dust storms add particles to the atmosphere. Erupting volcanoes spew out clouds of dust and ashes along with poisonous gases.

INTEGRATING HEALTH Even fairly clean air usually contains particles of dust and pollen. Figure 6 shows pollen, a fine, powdery material produced by many plants. The wind carries pollen not only to other plants, but also to people. One type of allergy, popularly called "hay fever," is caused by pollen from plants such as ragweed. Symptoms of hay fever include sneezing, a runny nose, red and itchy eyes, and headaches. Weather reports often include a "pollen count," which is the average number of pollen grains in a cubic meter of air.

Human Activities When people burn fuels such as wood and coal, particles made mostly of carbon enter the air. These particles of soot are what gives smoke its dark color. Farming and construction also release large amounts of soil particles into the air.

Figure 7 These people in Pontianak, Indonesia, are being given dust masks to protect them from smoke caused by widespread forest fires. *Inferring What effects do you think this smoke might have had on the people who live in this area?*

Sharpen your Skills

Predicting

Are the amounts of pollutants in the air always at the same level, or do they change from time to time? At what time of the day do you think the major sources of air pollution— cars, trucks, power plants, and factories— might produce the most pollution? Overall, do you think there is more air pollution in the morning or in the evening? On Mondays or on Fridays? On what did you base your prediction?

Smog

London-type smog forms when particles in coal smoke combine with water droplets in humid air. Fortunately, London-type smog is no longer common in the United States. Today sunny cities like Los Angeles often have another type of smog. The brown haze that forms in cities is called **photochemical smog**. The *photo-* in photochemical means "light." Photochemical smog is caused by the action of sunlight on chemicals.

INTEGRATING CHEMISTRY Photochemical smog is formed by a complex process. All fossil fuels contain hydrocarbons, which are substances composed of carbon and hydrogen. When fossil fuels are burned, some hydrocarbons are not burned completely and escape into the air. At the same time, the high temperatures that accompany burning cause some of the nitrogen in the air to react with oxygen to form nitrogen oxides. **The nitrogen oxides, hydrocarbons, and other air pollutants then react with each other in the presence of sunlight to form a mix of ozone and other chemicals called photochemical smog.** The ozone in photochemical smog irritates breathing passages, harms plants, and damages rubber, paint, and some plastics.

☑ *Checkpoint* How do natural conditions combine with human activities to create photochemical smog?

Acid Rain

One result of air pollution is acid rain. The burning of coal that contains a lot of sulfur produces substances composed of oxygen and sulfur called sulfur oxides. **Acid rain forms when nitrogen oxides and sulfur oxides combine with water in the air to form nitric acid and sulfuric acid.**

Figure 8 This scientist is studying trees damaged by acid rain. Acid rain is one of the results of air pollution.

Rain, sleet, snow, fog, and even dry particles carry these two acids from the air to trees, lakes, and buildings. Rain is naturally slightly acidic, but rain that contains more acid than normal is known as **acid rain.** Acid rain is sometimes strong enough to damage the surfaces of buildings and statues.

As Figure 8 shows, needle-leafed trees such as pines and spruce are especially sensitive to acid rain. Acid rain may make tree needles turn brown or fall off. It also harms lakes and ponds. Acid rain can make water so acidic that plants, amphibians, fish, and insects can no longer survive in it.

Improving Air Quality

The United States government and state governments have passed a number of laws and regulations to reduce air pollution. For example, pollution-control devices are required equipment on cars. Factories and power plants must install filters in smokestacks to remove pollutants from smoke before it is released into the atmosphere. These filters are called scrubbers.

Air quality in this country has generally improved over the past 30 years. The amounts of most major air pollutants have decreased. Newer cars cause less pollution than older models. Recently built power plants are less polluting than power plants that have been in operation for many years.

However, there are now more cars on the road and more power plants burning fossil fuels than in the past. Unfortunately, the air in many American cities is still polluted. Many people think that stricter regulations are needed to control air pollution. Others argue that reducing air pollution is very expensive and that the benefits of stricter regulations may not be worth the costs.

Section 2 Review

1. How is most air pollution produced?
2. Name two natural and two artificial sources of particles in the atmosphere.
3. How is photochemical smog formed? What kinds of harm does it cause?
4. What substances combine to form acid rain?
5. **Thinking Critically** Inferring Do you think that photochemical smog levels are higher during the winter or during the summer? Explain.

Science at Home

It's easy to see particles in the air. Gather your family members in a dark room. Open a window shade or blind slightly, or turn on a flashlight. Can they see tiny particles suspended in the beam of light? Discuss with your family where the particles came from. What might be some natural sources? What might be some human sources?

Cars and Clean Air

New technology and strict laws have brought cleaner air to many American cities. But in some places the air is still polluted. Cars and trucks still cause about half the air pollution in cities. And there are more cars on the road every year!

Worldwide, there are about 500 million cars. More cars will mean more pollution and more traffic jams. Unfortunately, cars stuck in traffic produce three times as much pollution as cars on the open road. What can people do to reduce air pollution by cars?

The Issues

Can Cars Be Made To Pollute Less?

In the past 20 years, cars have become more fuel-efficient and pollution levels have been lowered. Now engineers are running out of ways to make cars run more efficiently and produce less pollution. But technology does offer other answers.

Some vehicles use fuels other than gasoline. For instance, natural gas can power cars and trucks. Burning natural gas produces less pollution than burning gasoline.

Battery-powered electric cars produce no air pollution. However, the electricity to charge the batteries often comes from power plants that burn oil or coal. So electric cars still produce some pollution indirectly. Car makers have produced a few electric cars, but they are expensive and can make only fairly short trips.

Should People Drive Less?

Many car trips are shorter than a mile—an easy distance for most people to walk. For longer trips, people might consider riding a bicycle. Many cars on the road carry just one person. Some people might consider riding with others in car pools or taking buses or subways.

Are Stricter Standards or Taxes the Answer?

Some state governments have led efforts to reduce pollution. The state of California, for example, has strict anti-pollution laws. These laws set standards for gradually reducing pollutants released by cars. Stricter laws might make some old cars illegal.

Another approach is to make driving more expensive so that people use their cars less. That might mean higher gasoline taxes or fees for using the roads at busy times.

You Decide

1. Identify the Problem
In your own words, explain why automobiles make it hard to improve air quality. What kinds of pollution are caused by automobiles?

2. Analyze the Options
What are some ways to reduce the pollution caused by cars? Should these actions be voluntary, or should governments require them?

3. Find a Solution
How would you encourage people to try to reduce the pollution from cars? Create a visual essay from newspaper and magazine clippings. Write captions to explain your solution.

SECTION 3 Air Pressure

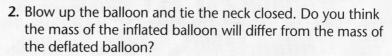

DISCOVER

Does Air Have Mass?

1. Use a balance to find the mass of a deflated balloon.

2. Blow up the balloon and tie the neck closed. Do you think the mass of the inflated balloon will differ from the mass of the deflated balloon?

3. Find the mass of the inflated balloon. Compare this mass to the mass of the deflated balloon. Was your prediction correct?

Think It Over

Drawing Conclusions Did the mass of the balloon change after it was inflated? What can you conclude about whether air has mass?

One of the best parts of eating roasted peanuts is opening the jar. When a jar of peanuts is "vacuum packed," most of the air is pumped out, creating low pressure inside. When you break the seal, the "whoosh" you hear is air from the outside rushing into the jar. The "whoosh" is the result of a difference in pressure between the outside of the jar and the inside.

Properties of Air

It may seem to you that air has no mass. However, air consists of atoms and molecules, which have mass. So air must have mass. **Because air has mass, it also has other properties, including density and pressure.**

Density The amount of mass in a given volume of air is its **density.** You can calculate density by dividing mass by volume.

$$Density = \frac{Mass}{Volume}$$

If there are more molecules in a given volume of air, the density is greater. If there are fewer molecules, the density decreases.

Pressure The force pushing on an area or surface is known as **pressure.** A denser substance has more mass per unit volume than a less dense one. So denser air exerts more pressure than less dense air.

To understand pressure, think of carrying a heavy backpack. The weight presses the straps into your shoulders just as the pack does to the hiker in the photo.

GUIDE FOR READING

◆ What are some of the properties of air?

◆ What instruments are used to measure air pressure?

◆ How does increasing altitude affect air pressure and density?

Reading Tip As you read this section, use the headings to make an outline about air pressure.

When you take off a backpack, it feels as if all the pressure has been taken off your shoulders. But has it? The weight of the column of air above you remains, as shown in Figure 9.

Air pressure is the result of the weight of a column of air pushing down on an area. The weight of the column of air above your desk is about the same as the weight of a large school bus! So why doesn't air pressure crush your desk? The reason is that the molecules in air push in all directions—down, up, and sideways. So the air pushing down on the top of your desk is balanced by the air pushing up on the bottom of the desk.

Figure 9 There is a column of air above you all the time. The weight of the air in the atmosphere causes air pressure.

Measuring Air Pressure

Have you ever heard a weather report say that the air pressure is falling? Falling air pressure usually indicates that a storm is approaching. Rising air pressure usually means that the weather is clearing. A **barometer** (buh RAHM uh tur) is an instrument that is used to measure changes in air pressure. **There are two kinds of barometers: mercury barometers and aneroid barometers.**

Mercury Barometers The first barometers invented were mercury barometers. Figure 10 shows how a mercury barometer works. A **mercury barometer** consists of a glass tube open at the bottom end and partially filled with mercury. The space in the tube above the mercury is almost a vacuum—it contains no air. The open end of the tube rests in a dish of mercury. The air pressure pushing down on the surface of the mercury in the dish is equal to the

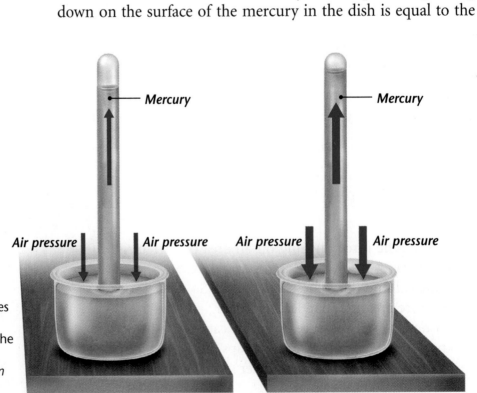

Mercury

Mercury

Air pressure   Air pressure   Air pressure   Air pressure

Figure 10 Air pressure pushes down on the surface of the mercury in the dish, causing the mercury in the tube to rise. *Predicting What happens when the air pressure increases?*

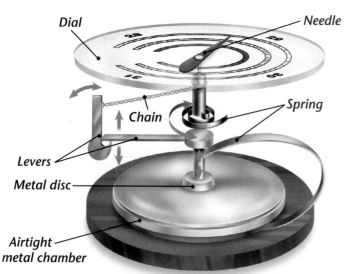

Dial

Needle

Spring

Chain

Levers

Metal disc

Airtight
metal chamber

Figure 11 Changes in air pressure cause the walls of the airtight metal chamber to flex in and out. The needle on the dial indicates the air pressure.

weight of the column of mercury in the tube. At sea level the mercury column is about 76 centimeters high, on average.

When the air pressure increases, it presses down more on the surface of the mercury. Greater air pressure forces the column of mercury higher. What will happen to the column of mercury if the air pressure decreases? The column will fall.

Aneroid Barometers If you have a barometer on a desk or wall at home, it is probably an aneroid barometer. The word *aneroid* means "without liquid." An **aneroid barometer** (AN uh royd) has an airtight metal chamber, as shown in Figure 11. The metal chamber is sensitive to changes in air pressure. When air pressure increases, the thin walls of the chamber are pushed in. When the pressure drops, the walls bulge out. The chamber is connected to a dial by a series of springs and levers. As the shape of the chamber changes, the needle on the dial moves.

Aneroid barometers are smaller than mercury barometers and don't contain a liquid. Therefore, they are portable and often more practical for uses such as airplane instrument panels.

Units of Air Pressure Weather reports use several different units for air pressure. Most weather reports for the general public use inches of mercury. For example, if the column of mercury in a mercury barometer is 30 inches high, the air pressure is "30 inches of mercury" or just "30 inches."

National Weather Service maps indicate air pressure in millibars. One inch of mercury equals approximately 33.87 millibars, so 30 inches of mercury is approximately equal to 1,016 millibars.

☑ *Checkpoint* *Name two common units used to measure air pressure.*

Soda-Bottle Barometer

Here's how to build a device that shows changes in air pressure.

1. Fill a 2-liter soda bottle one-half full with water.

2. Lower a long straw into the bottle so that the end of the straw is in the water. Seal the mouth of the bottle around the straw with modeling clay.

3. Squeeze the sides of the bottle. What happens to the level of the water in the straw?

4. Let go of the sides of the bottle. Watch the level of the water in the straw.

Inferring Explain your results in terms of air pressure.

Increasing Altitude

The air pressure at the top of Alaska's Mount McKinley—more than 6 kilometers above sea level—is less than half the air pressure at sea level. **Altitude,** or elevation, is the distance above sea level, the average level of the surface of the oceans. **Air pressure decreases as altitude increases. As air pressure decreases, so does density.**

Altitude Affects Air Pressure Imagine a stack of ten books. Which book has more weight on it, the second book from the top or the book at the bottom? The second book from the top has only the weight of one book on top of it. The book at the bottom

Working Under Pressure

Air pressure changes are related to changing weather conditions. In this lab, you will build and use your own barometer to measure air pressure.

Problem

How can a barometer detect changes in air pressure?

Materials

modeling clay · scissors
white glue · tape
pencil · wide-mouthed glass jar
metric ruler · rubber band
large rubber balloon
drinking straw, 12–15 cm long
cardboard strip, 10 cm x 25 cm

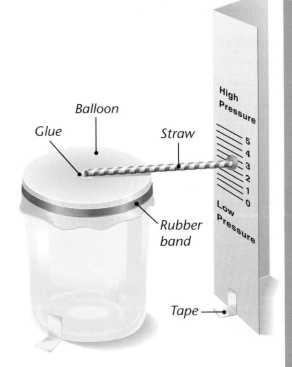

Glue · Balloon · Straw
High Pressure
5
4
3
2
1
0
Low Pressure
Rubber band
Tape

Procedure

1. Cut off the narrow opening of the balloon.
2. Fold the edges of the balloon outward. Carefully stretch the balloon over the open end of the glass jar. Use a rubber band to hold the balloon on the rim of the glass jar.

3. Place a small amount of glue on the center of the balloon top. Attach one end of the straw to the glue. Allow the other end to extend several centimeters beyond the edge of the glass jar. This is your pointer.

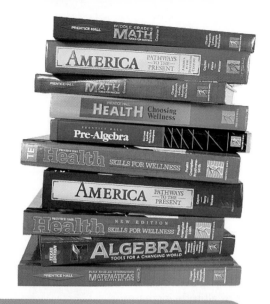

of the stack has the weight of all the other books pressing on it.

Air at sea level is like the bottom book. Recall that air pressure is the weight of the column of air pushing down on an area. Sea-level air has the weight of the whole atmosphere pressing on it. So air pressure is greatest at sea level. Air near the top of the atmosphere is like the second book from the top. There, the air has less weight pressing on it, and thus has lower air pressure.

DATA TABLE

Date and Time	Air Pressure	Weather Conditions

4. While the glue dries, fold the cardboard strip lengthwise and draw a scale along the edge with marks 0.5 cm apart. Write "High pressure" at the top of your scale and "Low pressure" at the bottom.
5. After the glue dries, add a pea-sized piece of modeling clay to the end of the pointer. Place your barometer and its scale in a location that is as free from temperature changes as possible. Arrange the scale and the barometer as shown in the diagram. Note that the pointer of the straw must just reach the cardboard strip.
6. Tape both the scale and the barometer to a surface so they do not move during your experiment.

7. In your notebook, make a data table like the one at the left. Record the date and time. Note the level of the straw on the cardboard strip.
8. Check the barometer twice a day. Record your observations in your data table.
9. Record the weather conditions for each day.

Analyze and Conclude

1. What change in atmospheric conditions must occur to cause the free end of the straw to rise? What change must occur for it to fall?
2. According to your observations, what kind of weather is usually associated with high air pressure? With low air pressure?
3. If the balloon had a tiny hole in it, what would happen to the accuracy of your barometer?
4. **Think About It** What effect, if any, would a great temperature change have on the accuracy of your barometer?

More to Explore

Compare changes in air pressure shown by your barometer with high and low air pressure readings shown on newspaper weather maps during the same time period. How do your readings compare with the readings in the newspapers?

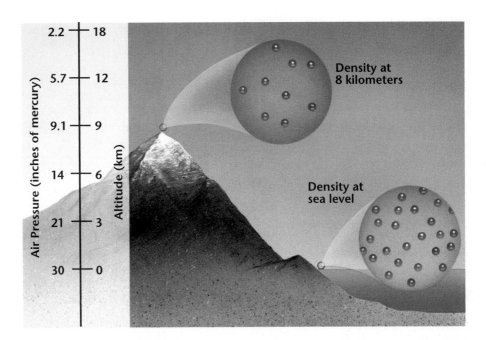

Figure 12 The density of air decreases as altitude increases. Air at sea level has more gas molecules in each cubic meter than air at the top of a mountain.

Altitude Also Affects Density If you were near the top
INTEGRATING
LIFE SCIENCE of Mount McKinley and tried to run, you would get out of breath quickly. Why would you have difficulty breathing at high altitudes?

As you go up through the atmosphere, the air pressure decreases. As air pressure decreases, the density of the air decreases. So density decreases as altitude increases, as shown in Figure 12.

Whether air is at sea level or at 6 kilometers above sea level, the air still contains 21 percent oxygen. However, since the air is less dense at a high altitude, there are fewer oxygen molecules to breathe in each cubic meter of air than there are at sea level. You are taking in less oxygen with each breath. That is why you get out of breath quickly.

Section 3 Review ## Science at Home

1. How does increasing the density of a gas affect its pressure?
2. Describe how a mercury barometer measures air pressure.
3. Why is the air at the top of a mountain hard to breathe?
4. **Thinking Critically** Predicting What changes in air pressure would you expect to see if you carried a barometer down a mine shaft? Explain.

Here's how you can show your family that air has pressure. Fill a glass with water. Place a piece of heavy cardboard over the top of the glass. Hold the cardboard in place with one hand as you turn the glass upside down. **CAUTION:** *Be sure the cardboard does not bend.* Now remove your hand from the cardboard. What happens? Explain to your family that the cardboard doesn't fall because the air pressure pushing up on it is greater than the weight of the water pushing down.

4 Layers of the Atmosphere

DISCOVER • ACTIVITY

Is Air There?

1. Use a heavy rubber band to tightly secure a plastic bag over the top of a wide-mouthed jar.

2. Gently try to push the bag into the jar. What happens? Is the air pressure higher inside or outside of the bag?

3. Remove the rubber band and line the inside of the jar with the plastic bag. Use the rubber band to tightly secure the edges of the bag over the rim of the jar.

4. Gently try to pull the bag out of the jar with your fingertips. What happens? Is the air pressure higher inside or outside of the bag?

Think It Over

Predicting Explain your observations in terms of air pressure. How do you think differences in air pressure would affect a weather balloon as it traveled up through the atmosphere?

Imagine taking a trip upward into the atmosphere in a hot-air balloon. You begin on a warm beach near the ocean, at an altitude of 0 kilometers.

You hear a roar as the balloon's pilot turns up the burner to heat the air in the balloon. The balloon begins to rise, and Earth's surface gets farther and farther away. As the balloon rises to an altitude of 3 kilometers, you realize that the air is getting colder. As you continue to rise, the air gets colder and colder. At 6 kilometers you begin to have trouble breathing. The air is becoming less dense. It's time to go back down.

What if you could have continued your balloon ride up through the atmosphere? As you rose farther up through the atmosphere, the air pressure and temperature would change dramatically. **The four main layers of the atmosphere are classified according to changes in temperature. These layers are the troposphere, the stratosphere, the mesosphere, and the thermosphere.**

The Troposphere

You live in the inner, or lowest, layer of Earth's atmosphere, the **troposphere** (TROH puh sfeer). *Tropo-* means "turning" or "changing"; conditions in the troposphere are more variable than in the other layers. The troposphere is where Earth's weather occurs.

GUIDE FOR READING

◆ What are the characteristics of the main layers of the atmosphere?

Reading Tip Before you read, preview *Exploring Layers of the Atmosphere*. Make a list of unfamiliar words. Look for the meanings of these words as you read.

Figure 13 This weather balloon will carry a package of instruments to measure weather conditions high in the atmosphere. *Applying Concepts* Which is the first layer of the atmosphere the balloon passes through on its way up?

Although hot-air balloons cannot travel very high into the troposphere, other types of balloons can. To measure weather conditions, scientists launch weather balloons that carry instruments up into the atmosphere. The balloons are not fully inflated before they are launched. Recall that air pressure decreases as you rise through the atmosphere. Leaving the balloon only partly inflated gives the gas inside the balloon room to expand as the air pressure outside the balloon decreases.

The depth of the troposphere varies from more than 16 kilometers above the equator to less than 9 kilometers above the North and South Poles. Even though it is the shallowest layer of the atmosphere, the troposphere contains almost all of the mass of the atmosphere.

As altitude increases in the troposphere, the temperature decreases. On average, for every 1-kilometer increase in altitude the air gets about 6.5 Celsius degrees cooler. At the top of the troposphere, the temperature stops decreasing and stays constant at about –60°C. Water here forms thin, feathery clouds of ice.

Checkpoint Why are clouds at the top of the troposphere made of ice crystals instead of drops of water?

The Stratosphere

The **stratosphere** extends from the top of the troposphere to about 50 kilometers above Earth's surface. *Strato-* is similar to *stratum*, which means "layer" or "spreading out."

The lower stratosphere is cold, about −60°C. You might be surprised to find out that the upper stratosphere is warmer than the lower stratosphere. Why is this? The upper stratosphere contains a layer of ozone, the three-atom form of oxygen. When the ozone in the stratosphere absorbs energy from the sun, the energy is converted into heat, warming the air.

As a weather balloon rises through the stratosphere, the air pressure outside the balloon continues to decrease. The volume of the balloon increases. Finally, the balloon bursts, and the instrument package falls back to Earth's surface.

The Mesosphere

Above the stratosphere, a drop in temperature marks the beginning of the next layer, the **mesosphere.** *Meso-* means "middle," so the mesosphere is the middle layer of the atmosphere. The mesosphere begins 50 kilometers above Earth's surface and ends at 80 kilometers. In the outer mesosphere temperatures approach −90°C.

EXPLORING Layers of the Atmosphere

The atmosphere is divided into four layers: the troposphere, the stratosphere, the mesosphere, and the thermosphere. The thermosphere is further divided into the ionosphere and the exosphere.

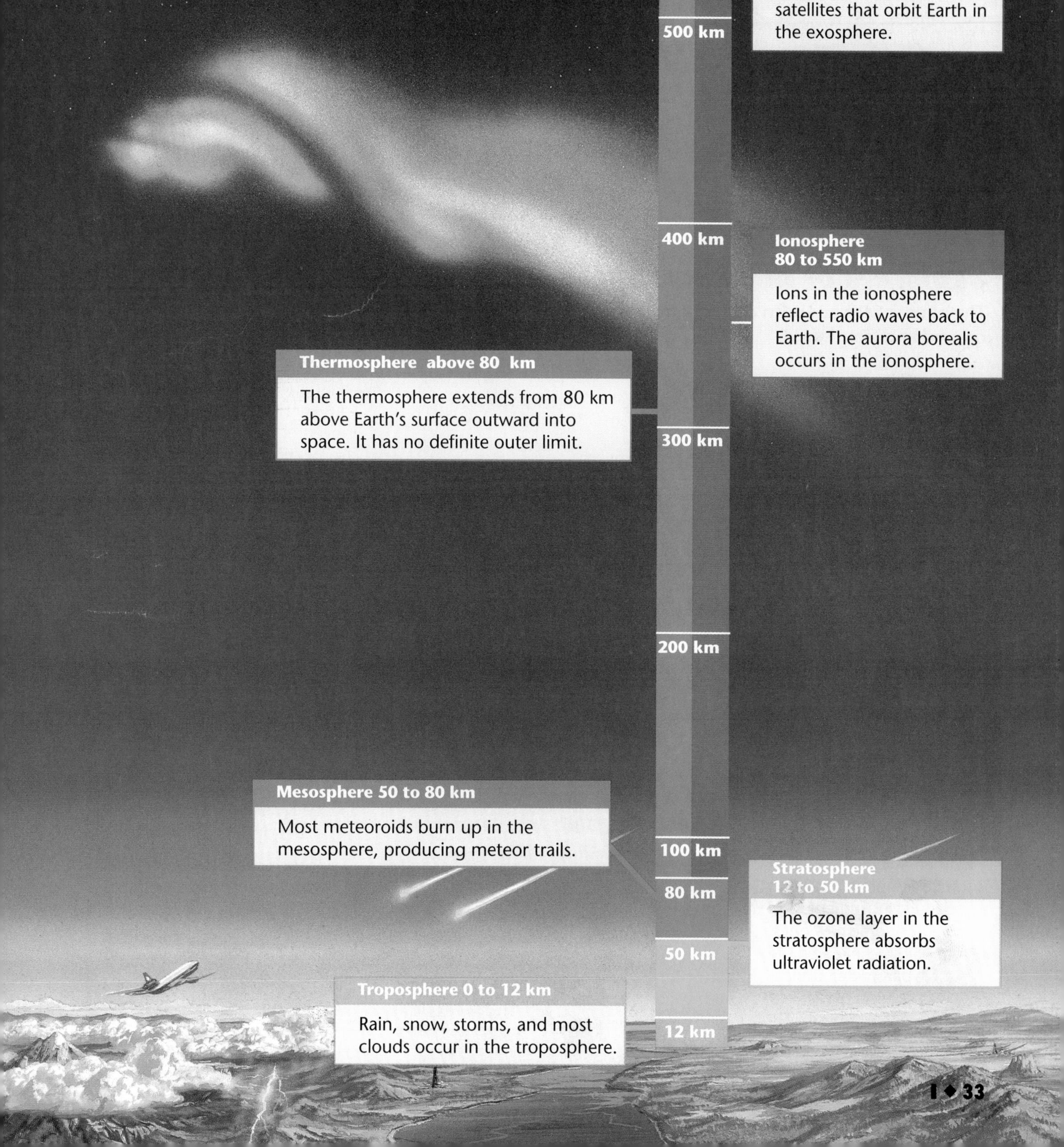

Exosphere above 550 km

Phone calls and television pictures often reach you by way of communications satellites that orbit Earth in the exosphere.

Ionosphere 80 to 550 km

Ions in the ionosphere reflect radio waves back to Earth. The aurora borealis occurs in the ionosphere.

Thermosphere above 80 km

The thermosphere extends from 80 km above Earth's surface outward into space. It has no definite outer limit.

Mesosphere 50 to 80 km

Most meteoroids burn up in the mesosphere, producing meteor trails.

Stratosphere 12 to 50 km

The ozone layer in the stratosphere absorbs ultraviolet radiation.

Troposphere 0 to 12 km

Rain, snow, storms, and most clouds occur in the troposphere.

550 km
500 km
400 km
300 km
200 km
100 km
80 km
50 km
12 km

INTEGRATING SPACE SCIENCE If you watch a shooting star streak across the night sky, you are seeing a meteoroid burn up as it enters the mesosphere. The mesosphere protects Earth's surface from being hit by most meteoroids, which are chunks of stone and metal from space. What you see as a shooting star, or meteor, is the trail of hot, glowing gases the burning meteoroid leaves behind.

☑ *Checkpoint* **What is the depth of the mesosphere?**

The Thermosphere

Near the top of the atmosphere, the air is very thin. The air 80 kilometers above Earth's surface is only about 0.001 percent as dense as the air at sea level. It's as though you took a cubic

SCIENCE & History

Explorers of the Atmosphere

The atmosphere has been explored from the ground and from space.

1746
Franklin's Experiment with Electricity

American statesman and inventor Benjamin Franklin and some friends in Philadelphia experimented with electricity in the atmosphere. To demonstrate that lightning is a form of electricity, Franklin flew a kite in a thunderstorm. However, Franklin did not hold the kite string in his hand, as this historical print shows.

| 1600 | 1700 | 1800 |

1643
Torricelli Invents the Barometer

Italian physicist and mathematician Evangelista Torricelli improved existing scientific instruments and invented some new ones. In 1643 he invented the barometer, using a column of mercury 1.2 meters high.

1804
Gay-Lussac Studies the Upper Troposphere

French chemist Joseph-Louis Gay-Lussac ascended to a height of about 7 kilometers in a hydrogen balloon to study the upper troposphere. Gay-Lussac studied pressure, temperature, and humidity.

meter of air at sea level and expanded it into 100,000 cubic meters at the top of the mesosphere. The outermost layer of the atmosphere, the **thermosphere**, extends from 80 kilometers above Earth's surface outward into space. It has no definite outer limit. The atmosphere does not end suddenly at the outer edge of the thermosphere. Gas atoms and molecules there are so far apart that the air blends gradually with outer space.

The *thermo-* in thermosphere means "heat." Even though the air in the thermosphere is thin, it is very hot, up to 1,800°C. The temperature in the thermosphere is actually higher than the temperature in a furnace used to make steel! But why is the thermosphere so hot? Energy coming from the sun strikes the thermosphere first. Nitrogen and oxygen molecules convert energy from the sun into heat.

In Your Journal

Imagine you were one of the first people to go up into the atmosphere in a balloon. What would you need to take? Find out what the early explorers took with them in their balloons. Write at least two paragraphs about what you would take, and why.

1931
Piccard Explores the Stratosphere

Swiss-Belgian physicist Auguste Piccard made the first ascent into the stratosphere. He reached a height of about 16 kilometers in an airtight cabin attached to a huge hydrogen balloon. Piccard is shown here with the cabin.

1900

2000

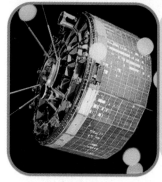

1960
First Weather Satellite Launched

TIROS-1, the first weather satellite equipped with a camera to send data back to Earth, was put into orbit by the United States. As later weather satellites circled Earth, they observed cloud cover and recorded temperatures and air pressures in the atmosphere.

1994
Space Shuttle Investigates the Atmosphere

The NASA space shuttle *Atlantis* traveled to a height of 300 kilometers in the thermosphere. *Atlantis* carried the ATLAS–3 research program, which observed the sun's influence on the atmosphere.

Figure 14 The aurora borealis, seen from Fairbanks, Alaska, creates a spectacular display in the night sky.

Despite the high temperature, however, you would not feel warm in the thermosphere. An ordinary thermometer would show a temperature well below 0°C. Why is that? Temperature is the average amount of energy of motion of each molecule of a substance. The gas molecules in the thermosphere move very rapidly, so the temperature is very high. However, the molecules are spaced far apart in the thin air. And there are not enough of them to collide with a thermometer and warm it very much. So an ordinary thermometer would not detect the molecules' energy.

The Ionosphere The thermosphere is divided into two layers. The lower layer of the thermosphere, called the **ionosphere** (eye AHN uh sfeer), begins 80 kilometers above the surface and ends at 550 kilometers. Energy from the sun causes gas molecules in the ionosphere to become electrically charged particles called ions. Radio waves bounce off ions in the ionosphere and then bounce back to Earth's surface.

The brilliant light displays of the **aurora borealis**—the Northern Lights—also occur in the ionosphere. The aurora borealis is caused by particles from the sun that enter the ionosphere near the North Pole. These particles strike oxygen and nitrogen atoms in the ionosphere, causing them to glow.

The Exosphere *Exo-* means "outer," so the **exosphere** is the

INTEGRATING TECHNOLOGY outer layer of the thermosphere. The exosphere extends from 550 kilometers outward for thousands of kilometers. When you make a long-distance phone call or watch television, the signal may have traveled up to a satellite orbiting in the exosphere and then back down to your home. Satellites are also used for watching the world's weather and carrying telescopes that look deep into space.

Section 4 Review

1. Describe one characteristic of each of the four main layers of the atmosphere.
2. What is a shooting star? In which layer of the atmosphere would you see it?
3. What is the aurora borealis? In which layer of the atmosphere does it occur?
4. **Thinking Critically Drawing Conclusions** Why is the mesosphere the coldest part of the atmosphere?

Check Your Progress CHAPTER PROJECT 1
At this point, review your weather log. What do you notice about the weather on one day that might allow you to predict the next day's weather? What weather conditions changed the most from day to day? Continue to record your observations and start thinking about how you will present them.

SECTION **1 The Air Around You**

Key Ideas
◆ Earth's atmosphere makes conditions on Earth suitable for living things.
◆ Earth's atmosphere is made up of molecules of nitrogen, oxygen, carbon dioxide, and water vapor, as well as some other gases and particles of liquids and solids.

Key Terms
weather   ozone
atmosphere   water vapor

 SECTION **2 Air Quality**

INTEGRATING ENVIRONMENTAL SCIENCE

Key Ideas
◆ Most air pollution results from the burning of fossil fuels such as coal and oil.
◆ Nitrogen oxides, hydrocarbons, and other air pollutants react with one another in the presence of sunlight to form a mix of ozone and other chemicals called photochemical smog.
◆ Acid rain forms when nitrogen oxides and sulfur oxides combine with water in the air to form nitric acid and sulfuric acid.

Key Terms
pollutant   acid rain
photochemical smog

 SECTION **3 Air Pressure**

Key Ideas
◆ Properties of air include mass, density, and pressure.
◆ Air pressure is the result of the weight of a column of air pushing down on an area.
◆ Air pressure is measured with mercury barometers and aneroid barometers.
◆ Air pressure decreases as altitude increases. As air pressure decreases, so does density.

Key Terms
density   barometer   altitude
pressure   mercury barometer
air pressure aneroid barometer

SECTION **4 Layers of the Atmosphere**

Key Ideas
◆ The four main layers of the atmosphere are classified according to changes in temperature. These layers are the troposphere, the stratosphere, the mesosphere, and the thermosphere.
◆ Rain, snow, storms, and most clouds occur in the troposphere.
◆ Ozone in the stratosphere absorbs energy from the sun.
◆ Most meteoroids burn up in the mesosphere, producing meteor trails.
◆ The aurora borealis occurs in the ionosphere.
◆ Communications satellites orbit Earth in the exosphere.

Key Terms
troposphere   thermosphere   aurora borealis
stratosphere   ionosphere   exosphere
mesosphere

Organizing Information

Concept Map Copy the air pressure concept map onto a separate sheet of paper. Then complete it and add a title. (For more on concept maps, see the Skills Handbook.)

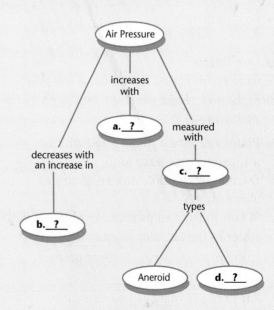

Reviewing Content

 For more review of key concepts, see the Interactive Student Tutorial CD-ROM.

Multiple Choice

Choose the letter of the answer that best completes each statement.

1. The most abundant gas in the atmosphere is
   a. ozone.   b. carbon dioxide.
   c. oxygen.   d. nitrogen.
2. Most air pollution is caused by
   a. dust and pollen.
   b. acid rain.
   c. erupting volcanoes.
   d. the burning of fossil fuels.
3. A barometer is used to measure
   a. temperature.   b. smog.
   c. air pressure   d. density.
4. The layers of the atmosphere are classified according to changes in
   a. altitude.
   b. temperature.
   c. pressure.
   d. density.
5. The inner layer, or "weather layer," of the atmosphere is called the
   a. mesosphere.
   b. troposphere.
   c. thermosphere.
   d. stratosphere.

True or False

If the statement is true, write true. If it is false, change the underlined word or words to make the statement true.

6. Plants need <u>carbon dioxide</u> from the atmosphere to make food.
7. Burning fuels add <u>nitrogen</u> to the atmosphere.
8. When sulfur and nitrogen oxides mix with water in the air, they form <u>smog</u>.
9. If the mass of a fixed volume of air increases, it becomes <u>less</u> dense.
10. Air pressure <u>increases</u> as you climb from land at sea level to the top of a mountain.

Checking Concepts

11. Name two ways in which carbon dioxide is added to the atmosphere.
12. Explain why it is difficult to include water vapor in a graph that shows the percentages of various gases in the atmosphere.
13. What is the difference between photochemical smog and London-type smog?
14. Describe some of the problems caused by acid rain.
15. List the following layers of the atmosphere in order moving up from Earth's surface: thermosphere, stratosphere, troposphere, mesosphere.
16. Describe the temperature changes that occur as you move upward through the troposphere.
17. **Writing to Learn** You are a scientist who has a chance to join a research mission to explore the atmosphere. To win a place on this mission, write a persuasive letter telling which layer of the atmosphere you want to research and why you chose it.

Thinking Critically

18. **Predicting** Describe the changes in the atmosphere that you would experience while climbing a mountain four or more kilometers high. How might these changes affect you physically?
19. **Applying Concepts** Why can an aneroid barometer be used to measure elevation as well as air pressure?
20. **Relating Cause and Effect** How can burning high-sulfur coal in a power-generating plant harm a forest hundreds of kilometers away?
21. **Classifying** Which sources of air pollution occur naturally, and which are caused by humans?

Applying Skills

The table below shows the temperature at various altitudes above Omaha, Nebraska, on a day in January. Use the table to answer the questions that follow.

Altitude (kilometers)	0	1.6	3.2	4.8	6.4	7.2
Temperature (°C)	0	–4	–9	–21	–32	–40

22. **Graphing** Make a line graph of the data in the table. Put temperature on the horizontal axis and altitude on the vertical axis. Label your graph.

23. **Interpreting Graphs** At about what height above the ground was the temperature –15°C?

24. **Interpreting Graphs** What was the approximate temperature 2.4 kilometers over Omaha?

25. **Calculating** Suppose an airplane was about 6.8 kilometers above Omaha on this day. What was the approximate temperature at 6.8 kilometers? How much colder was the temperature at 6.8 kilometers above the ground than at ground level?

Performance   CHAPTER PROJECT 1   Assessment

Project Wrap Up For your class presentation, prepare a display of your weather observations. Include drawings, graphs, and tables that summarize the weather you observed. Practice presenting your project to your group. Do you need to make any improvements? If so, make them now.

Reflect and Record In your journal, write how you might improve your weather log. What weather conditions would you like to know more about? What factors could you have measured more accurately using instruments?

Test Preparation

Use these questions to prepare for standardized tests.

Study the graph. Then answer Questions 26–29.

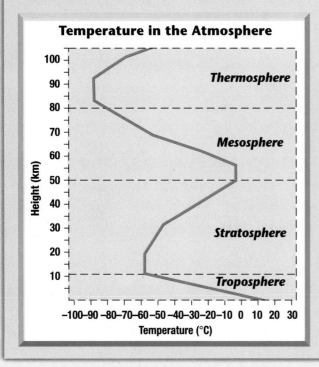

26. Name the layer of the atmosphere that is closest to Earth's surface.
   a. thermosphere   b. troposphere
   c. stratosphere   d. mesosphere

27. Which layer of the atmosphere has the lowest temperature?
   a. thermosphere   b. troposphere
   c. stratosphere   d. mesosphere

28. The range of temperatures found in the stratosphere is about ____ Celsius degrees.
   a. 100   b. 0
   c. 30   d. 60

29. Which of the following best describes how temperature changes as altitude increases in the troposphere?
   a. steadily increases
   b. increases then decreases
   c. steadily decreases
   d. decreases then increases

CHAPTER 2 Weather Factors

WEB ACTIVITY 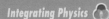 www.phschool.com

PROJECT 2

Your Own Weather Station

A drenching spring rain is just what the flowers need! As the weather gets warmer, the garden will bloom. Warm days, soft winds, and plenty of rain—all of these are weather factors that affect growing things. In this chapter, you will learn about a variety of weather factors, including air pressure, temperature, wind speed and direction, relative humidity, precipitation, and the amount and types of clouds.

Your Goal To measure and record weather conditions using instruments. You will look for patterns in your data that can be used to predict the next day's weather.

In completing your project, you will
◆ develop a plan for measuring weather factors
◆ record your data in a daily log
◆ display your data in a set of graphs
◆ use your data and graphs to try to predict the weather
◆ follow the safety guidelines in Appendix A

Get Started Begin by previewing the chapter to see what weather factors you want to measure. Discuss with a group of your classmates what instruments you might use. Brainstorm what observations you should make each day.

Check Your Progress You'll be working on the project as you study this chapter. To keep your project on track, look for Check Your Progress boxes at the following points.

Section 2 Review, page 51: Prepare to make observations.
Section 3 Review, page 60: Collect and record data.
Section 5 Review, page 70: Graph your data and look for patterns.

Wrap Up At the end of the chapter (page 73), present your weather observations and explain how well you predicted the weather.

Spring rains are an important factor in helping these tulips grow.

SECTION 4 **Water in the Atmosphere**

Discover **How Does Fog Form?**
Sharpen Your Skills **Interpreting Data**

SECTION 5 **Precipitation**

Discover **How Can You Make Hail?**
Sharpen Your Skills **Calculating**

SECTION 1 Energy in the Atmosphere

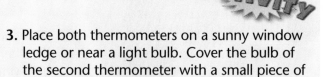

DISCOVER

Does a Plastic Bag Trap Heat?

1. Record the initial temperatures on two thermometers. (You should get the same readings.)

2. Place one of the thermometers in a plastic bag. Put a small piece of paper in the bag so that it shades the bulb of the thermometer. Seal the bag.

3. Place both thermometers on a sunny window ledge or near a light bulb. Cover the bulb of the second thermometer with a small piece of paper. Predict what you think will happen.

4. Wait five minutes. Then record the temperatures on the two thermometers.

Think It Over

Measuring Were the two temperatures the same? How could you explain any difference?

GUIDE FOR READING

◆ In what form does energy from the sun travel to Earth?

◆ What happens to energy from the sun when it reaches Earth?

Reading Tip Before you read, skim the section for boldfaced words that are unfamiliar to you. As you read, find their meanings and write them down in your notebook.

Think of a sunny summer day. When you get up in the morning, the sun is low in the sky and the air is cool. As the sun rises, the temperature increases. By noon it is quite hot. As you will see in this chapter, heat is a major factor in the weather. The movement of heat in the atmosphere causes temperatures to change, winds to blow, and rain to fall.

Energy from the Sun

 INTEGRATING PHYSICS Nearly all the energy in Earth's atmosphere comes from the sun. This energy travels to Earth as **electromagnetic waves,** a form of energy that can travel through space. Electromagnetic waves are classified according to wavelength, or distance between waves. The direct transfer of energy by electromagnetic waves is called **radiation.**

Most of the energy from the sun reaches Earth in the form of visible light and infrared radiation, and a small amount of ultraviolet radiation. Visible light is a mixture of all of the colors that you see in a rainbow: red, orange, yellow, green, blue, and violet. The different colors are the result of different wavelengths

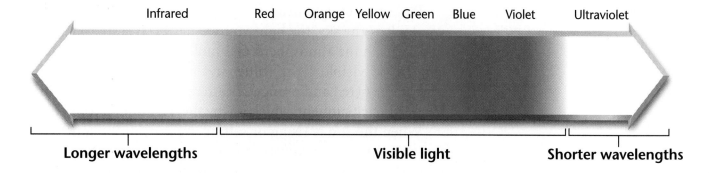

Infrared Red Orange Yellow Green Blue Violet Ultraviolet

Longer wavelengths   **Visible light**   **Shorter wavelengths**

of visible light. Red and orange light have the longest wavelengths, while blue and violet light have the shortest wavelengths.

Infrared radiation is a form of energy with wavelengths that are longer than red light. Infrared radiation is not visible, but can be felt as heat. Heat lamps used to keep food warm in restaurants give off both visible red light and invisible infrared radiation. The sun also gives off **ultraviolet radiation,** which has wavelengths that are shorter than violet light. Sunburns are caused by ultraviolet radiation. This radiation can also cause skin cancer and eye damage.

☑ *Checkpoint* *Which color of visible light has the longest wavelengths?*

Energy in the Atmosphere

Before the sun's rays can reach Earth's surface, they must pass through the atmosphere. The path of the sun's rays is shown in *Exploring Energy in the Atmosphere* on the following page.

Some of the energy from the sun is absorbed within the atmosphere. Water vapor and carbon dioxide absorb some infrared radiation. The ozone layer in the stratosphere absorbs most of the ultraviolet radiation. Clouds, dust, and other gases also absorb energy from the sun.

Some of the sun's rays are reflected. Clouds in the atmosphere act like mirrors, reflecting some solar energy back into space. In addition, dust particles and molecules of gases in the atmosphere reflect light from the sun in all directions.

Figure 1 Electromagnetic waves include infrared radiation, visible light, and ultraviolet radiation. *Interpreting Diagrams What type of radiation has wavelengths that are shorter than visible light? What type has wavelengths that are longer?*

Reflection of light in all directions is called **scattering.** When you look at the sky, the light you see has been scattered by gas molecules in the atmosphere. Gas molecules scatter short wavelengths of visible light (blue and violet) more than long wavelengths (red and orange). Scattered light is therefore bluer than ordinary sunlight, which is why the daytime sky looks blue.

When the sun is rising or setting, light from the sun passes through a greater thickness of the atmosphere than when the sun is higher in the sky. More light from the blue end of the spectrum is removed by scattering before it reaches your eyes. The remaining light from the sun contains mostly red and orange light. The sun looks red, and clouds around it become very colorful.

✓ *Checkpoint* *Why would particles from volcanic eruptions make sunsets and sunrises more red?*

EXPLORING *Energy in the Atmosphere*

Most of the energy that keeps Earth warm comes from the sun. Some of this energy is reflected or absorbed in the atmosphere. The rest of the energy reaches Earth's surface, where it is reflected or absorbed.

Solar energy is mostly visible light and infrared radiation, with a small amount of ultraviolet radiation.

Clouds, dust, and gases in the atmosphere reflect and scatter light.

Gases and particles in the atmosphere absorb solar energy.

Some energy that reaches the surface is reflected back into the atmosphere.

Earth's surface absorbs solar energy. This energy heats the land and water.

Some of the absorbed energy is then radiated back into the atmosphere.

Energy at Earth's Surface

Some of the sun's energy reaches Earth's surface and is reflected back into the atmosphere. Some of the energy, however, is absorbed by the land and water and changed into heat.

When Earth's surface is heated, it radiates some of the energy back into the atmosphere as infrared radiation. Most of this infrared radiation cannot travel all the way through the atmosphere back into space. Instead, much of it is absorbed by water vapor, carbon dioxide, methane, and other gases in the air. The energy from the absorbed radiation heats the gases in the air. These gases form a "blanket" around Earth that holds heat in the atmosphere. The process by which gases hold heat in the air is called the **greenhouse effect.**

Have you ever been inside a greenhouse during the winter? Even on a cold day, a greenhouse is warm. Greenhouses trap heat in two ways. First, infrared radiation given off in the interior cannot easily pass through glass and is trapped inside. Second, warm air inside the greenhouse cannot rise because the glass blocks the movement of air. What happens in Earth's atmosphere is similar to the first way that greenhouses trap heat.

The greenhouse effect is a natural process that keeps Earth's atmosphere at a temperature that is comfortable for most living things. Human activities over the last 200 years, however, have increased the amount of carbon dioxide in the atmosphere, which may be warming the atmosphere. You will learn more about the greenhouse effect in Chapter 4.

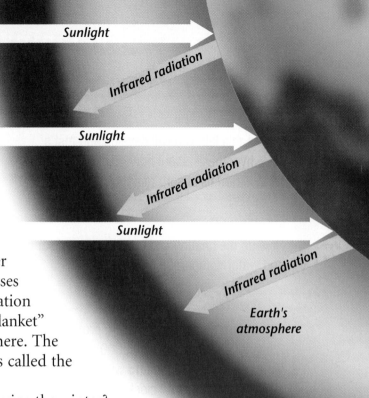

Figure 2 Sunlight travels through the atmosphere to Earth's surface. Earth's surface then gives off infrared radiation. Much of this energy is held by the atmosphere, warming it.

Section 1 Review

1. List three forms of radiation from the sun. How are these alike? How are they different?
2. What happens to the energy from the sun that is absorbed by Earth's surface?
3. Why is the sky blue? Why are sunsets often red?
4. **Thinking Critically** **Applying Concepts** What might conditions on Earth be like without the greenhouse effect?

Science at Home

With an adult family member, explore the role radiation plays in heating your home. Are some rooms warmer and sunnier in the morning? Are other rooms warmer and sunnier in the afternoon? How does opening and closing curtains or blinds affect the temperature of a room? Explain your observations to your family.

Heating Earth's Surface

I n this lab, you will develop and test a hypothesis about how quickly different materials absorb radiation.

Problem

How do the heating and cooling rates of sand and water compare?

Materials

2 thermometers or temperature probes
2 beakers, 400 mL   sand, 300 mL
water, 300 mL   lamp with 150-W bulb
metric ruler   clock or stopwatch
string   graph paper
ring stand and two ring clamps

Procedure

1. Do you think sand or water will heat up faster? Record your hypothesis. Then follow these steps to test your hypothesis.
2. Copy the data table into your notebook. Add enough rows to record data for 15 minutes.
3. Fill one beaker with 300 mL of dry sand.
4. Fill the second beaker with 300 mL of water at room temperature.
5. Arrange the beakers beneath the ring stand.
6. Place one thermometer in each beaker. If you are using a temperature probe, see your teacher for instructions.
7. Suspend the thermometers from the ring stand with string. This will hold the thermometers in place so they do not fall.

8. Adjust the height of the clamp so that the bulb of each thermometer is covered by about 0.5 cm of sand or water in a beaker.
9. Position the lamp so that it is about 20 cm above the sand and water. There should be no more than 8 cm between the beakers. **CAUTION:** *Be careful not to splash water onto the hot light bulb.*
10. Record the temperature of the sand and water in your data table.
11. Turn on the lamp. Read the temperature of the sand and water every minute for 15 minutes. Record the temperatures in the Light On column in the data table.
12. Which material do you think will cool off more quickly? Record your hypothesis. Again, give reasons why you think your hypothesis is correct.
13. Turn the light off. Read the temperature of the sand and water every minute for another 15 minutes. Record the temperatures in the Light Off column (16–30 minutes).

DATA TABLE

Temperature with Light On (°C)			Temperature with Light Off (°C)		
Time (min)	Sand	Water	Time (min)	Sand	Water
Start			16		
1			17		
2			18		
3			19		
4			20		
5			21		

Analyze and Conclude

1. Draw two line graphs to show the data for the temperature change in sand and water over time. Label the horizontal axis from 0 to 30 minutes and the vertical axis in degrees Celsius. Draw both graphs on the same piece of graph paper. Use a dashed line to show the temperature change in water and a solid line to show the temperature change in sand.

2. Calculate the total change in temperature for each material.

3. Based on your data, which material had the greater increase in temperature?

4. What can you conclude about which material absorbed heat faster? How do your results compare with your hypothesis?

5. Review your data again. In 15 minutes, which material cooled faster?

6. How do these results compare to your second hypothesis?

7. **Think About It** If your results did not support either of your hypotheses, why do you think the results differed from what you expected?

8. **Apply** Based on your results, which do you think will heat up more quickly on a sunny day: the water in a lake or the sand surrounding it? Which will cool off more quickly after dark?

More to Explore

Do you think all solid materials heat up as fast as sand? For example, consider gravel, crushed stone, or different types of soil. Write a hypothesis about their heating rates as an "If . . . then. . . ." statement. With the approval and supervision of your teacher, develop a procedure to test your hypothesis. Was your hypothesis correct?

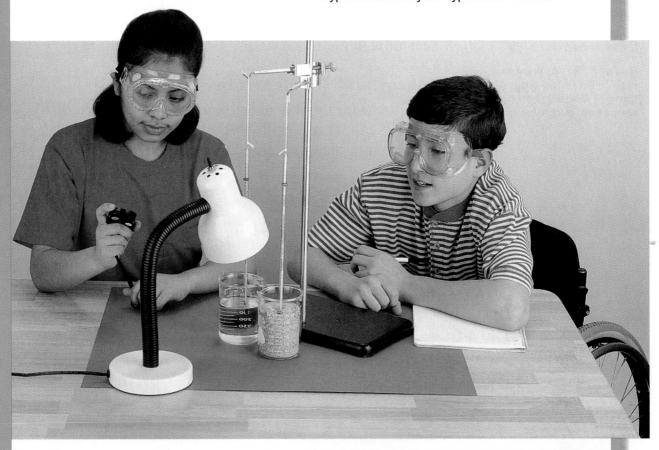

SECTION 2 Heat Transfer

DISCOVER

ACTIVITY

What Happens When Air Is Heated?

1. Use heavy scissors to cut the flat part out of an aluminum pie plate. Use the tip of the scissors to poke a small hole in the middle of the flat part.

2. Cut the part into a spiral shape, as shown in the photo. Tie a 30-centimeter piece of thread to the middle of the spiral.

3. Hold the spiral over a source of heat, such as a candle, hot plate, or incandescent light bulb.

Think It Over

Inferring What happened to the spiral? Why do you think this happened?

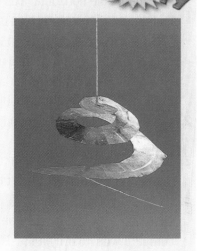

GUIDE FOR READING

◆ How is temperature measured?

◆ In what three ways is heat transferred?

Reading Tip As you read, make a list of the types of heat transfer. Write a sentence about how each type occurs.

You know that energy from the sun is absorbed by Earth's surface. Some energy is then transferred from the surface to the atmosphere in the form of heat. The heat then moves from place to place within the atmosphere. But how does heat move in the atmosphere?

Energy and Temperature

Gases are made up of small particles, called molecules, that are constantly moving. The faster the molecules are moving, the more energy they have. Figure 3 shows how the motion of

Figure 3 The lemonade is cold, so the molecules move slowly. The herbal tea is hot, so the molecules move faster than the molecules in the lemonade. *Inferring Which liquid has a higher temperature?*

molecules is related to the amount of energy they hold. The total energy of motion in the molecules of a substance is called **thermal energy.** On the other hand, **temperature** is the *average* amount of energy of motion of each molecule of a substance. That means that temperature is a measure of how hot or cold a substance is.

Measuring Temperature

Ask someone what the weather is like. The answer will probably include the temperature. Temperature is one of the most important elements of weather. **Air temperature is usually measured with a thermometer.** A **thermometer** is a thin glass tube with a bulb on one end that contains a liquid, usually mercury or colored alcohol.

Thermometers work because liquids expand when they are heated and contract when they are cooled. When the air temperature increases, the liquid in the bulb expands and rises up the column. What happens when the temperature decreases? The liquid in the bulb contracts and moves down the tube.

Temperature is measured in units called degrees. The two most common scales are shown in Figure 4. Scientists use the Celsius scale. On the Celsius scale, the freezing point of pure water is 0°C (read "zero degrees Celsius"). The boiling point of pure water is 100°C. Weather reports in the United States use the Fahrenheit scale. On the Fahrenheit scale, the freezing point of water is 32°F and the boiling point is 212°F.

Figure 4 Scientists use the Celsius scale to measure temperature. However, weather reports use the Fahrenheit scale. *Measuring According to this thermometer, what is the air temperature in degrees Celsius?*

☑ *Checkpoint* *How many degrees Celsius are there between the freezing point of water and the boiling point of water?*

How Heat Is Transferred

The energy transferred from a hotter object to a cooler one is referred to as **heat.** The types of heat transfer are shown in Figure 5 on the next page. **Heat is transferred in three ways: radiation, conduction, and convection.**

Radiation Have you ever felt the warmth of the sun's rays on your face? You were feeling energy coming directly from the sun as radiation. Recall that radiation is the direct transfer of energy by electromagnetic waves. The heat you feel from the sun or a campfire travels directly to you as infrared radiation. You cannot see infrared radiation, but you can feel it as heat.

Temperatures at Two Heights

How much difference do you think there is between air temperatures near the ground and air temperatures higher up? Give reasons for your prediction.

1. Take all of your measurements at a location that is sunny all day.

2. Early in the morning, measure the air temperature 1 cm and 1.25 m above the ground. Record the time of day and the temperature for both locations. Repeat your measurements late in the afternoon.

3. Record these measurements in the morning and afternoon for two more days.

4. Graph your data for each height with temperature on the vertical axis and time on the horizontal axis. Draw both lines on the same piece of graph paper using the same axes. Label both lines.

Interpreting Data At which height did the temperature vary the most? How can you explain the difference?

Conduction   Have you ever walked barefoot on hot sand? Your feet felt hot because heat moved directly from the sand into your feet. When a fast-moving molecule bumps into a nearby slower-moving molecule, it transfers some of its energy. The direct transfer of heat from one substance to another substance that it is touching is called **conduction.** The molecules that gain energy can in turn pass the energy along to other nearby molecules. When you walk on hot sand, the fast-moving molecules in the sand transfer heat into the slower-moving molecules in your feet.

The closer together the molecules in a substance are, the more effectively they can conduct heat. Conduction works well in some solids, such as metals, but not as well in liquids and gases. Air and water do not conduct heat very well.

Convection   How can you dry your boots over a hot-air vent, even though the furnace is in another room? Air from the furnace carries the heat to your boots. In fluids (liquids and gases), molecules can move from place to place. As the molecules move, they take their heat along with them. The transfer of heat by the movement of a fluid is called **convection.**

☑ *Checkpoint Give at least one example each of radiation, conduction, and convection in your daily life.*

Heat Transfer in the Troposphere

Radiation, conduction, and convection work together to heat the troposphere. When Earth's surface absorbs solar energy during the day, the surface of the land becomes warmer than the air. Air near Earth's surface is warmed by radiation and conduction of heat from the surface to the air. However, heat is not easily conducted from one air molecule to another. Only the first few meters of the troposphere are heated by conduction. Thus, the air close to the ground is usually warmer than the air a few meters up.

Convection causes most of the heating of the troposphere. When the air near the ground is heated, the molecules have more energy. Because they have more energy, the molecules move

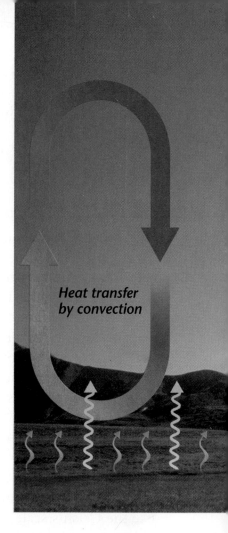

Heat transfer by convection

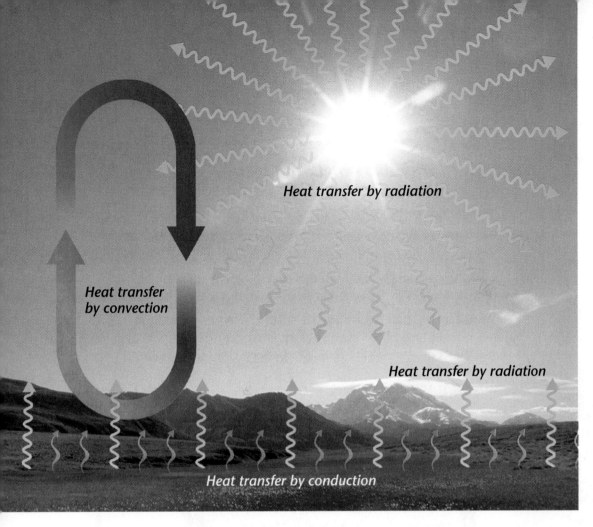

Heat transfer by radiation

Heat transfer
by convection

Heat transfer by radiation

Heat transfer by conduction

faster. As the molecules in the heated air move, they bump into each other and move farther apart. The air becomes less dense. Cooler, denser air sinks, forcing the warmer, less dense air to rise.

The upward movement of warm air and the downward movement of cool air form convection currents. Convection currents move heat throughout the troposphere.

Figure 5 All three types of heat transfer—radiation, convection, and conduction—occur near Earth's surface.

 Section 2 Review

1. What is temperature?
2. Describe how a thermometer works.
3. Name three ways that heat can be transferred. Briefly explain how the three work together to heat the troposphere.
4. **Thinking Critically Applying Concepts** When you light a fire in a fireplace, warm air rises by convection and goes up the chimney. How, then, does a fireplace heat a room? Why do only the people directly in front of the fireplace feel the warmth of the fire?

Check Your Progress

CHAPTER PROJECT 2

Gather the instruments you will need to measure the weather factors. (*Hint:* Make sure you know how to take accurate measurements.) Plan when and where to measure weather factors. Be sure to take your measurements at the same location and at the same time of day.

SECTION 3 Winds

DISCOVER · ACTIVITY · · ·

Which Way Does the Wind Turn?

Do this activity with a partner. Think of the ball as a model of Earth and the marker as representing wind.

1. Using heavy-duty tape, attach a pencil to a large smooth ball so that you can spin the ball from the top without touching it.

2. One partner should hold the pencil. Slowly turn the ball counterclockwise when seen from above.

3. While the ball is turning, the second partner should use a marker to try to draw a straight line from the "North Pole" to the "equator" of the ball. What shape does the line form?

Think It Over
Making Models If cold air were moving south from Canada into the United States, how would its movement be affected by Earth's rotation?

GUIDE FOR READING

◆ What causes winds?

◆ What are local winds and global winds?

◆ Where are the major global wind belts located?

Reading Tip Before you read, preview the illustrations and read their captions. Write down any questions you have about winds. As you read, look for answers to your questions.

The highest point in the northeastern United States, at 1,917 meters above sea level, is Mount Washington in New Hampshire. Sometimes winds near the top of this mountain are so strong that hikers cannot safely reach the summit! The greatest wind speed ever measured at Earth's surface—370 kilometers per hour—was measured on April 12, 1934, at the top of Mount Washington. What causes this incredible force?

What Causes Winds?

Because air is a fluid, it can move easily from place to place. The force that makes air move is caused by a difference of air pressure. Fluids tend to move from areas of high pressure to areas of low pressure. A **wind** is the horizontal movement of air from an area of high pressure to an area of lower pressure. **All winds are caused by differences in air pressure.**

Most differences in air pressure are caused by unequal heating of the atmosphere. As you learned in the previous section, convection currents form when an area of Earth's surface is heated by the sun's rays. Air over the heated surface expands and becomes less dense. As the air becomes less dense, its air pressure decreases. If a nearby area is not heated as much, the air above the less-heated area will be cooler and denser. The cool, dense air has a higher air pressure so it flows underneath the warm, less dense air. This process forces the warm air to rise.

Measuring Wind

Winds are described by their direction and speed. Wind direction is determined with a wind vane. The wind swings the wind vane so that one end points into the wind. The name of a wind tells you where the wind is coming from. For example, a south wind blows from the south toward the north. A north wind blows to the south.

Wind speed is measured with an **anemometer** (an uh MAHM uh tur). An anemometer has three or four cups mounted at the ends of spokes that spin on an axle. The force of the wind against the cups turns the axle. A speedometer attached to the axle shows the wind speed.

A cool breeze can be very refreshing on a warm day. However, during the winter, a similar breeze can make you feel uncomfortably cold. The wind blowing over your skin removes body heat. The stronger the wind, the colder you feel. The increased cooling that a wind can cause is called the **wind-chill factor**. Thus a weather report may say, "The temperature is 20 degrees Fahrenheit. But with a wind speed of 30 miles per hour, the wind-chill factor makes it feel like 18 degrees below zero."

☑ *Checkpoint* *Toward what direction does a west wind blow?*

Build a Wind Vane

Here's how to build your own wind vane.

1. ✂ Use scissors to cut out a pointer and a slightly larger tail fin from construction paper.

2. Make a slit 1 cm deep in each end of a soda straw.

3. Slide the pointer and tail fin into place on the straw, securing them with small pieces of tape.

4. Hold the straw on your finger to find the point at which it balances.

5. Carefully push a pin through the balance point and into the eraser of a pencil. Move the wind vane back and forth to make sure it can spin freely.

Observing How can you use your wind vane to tell the direction of the wind?

Figure 6 The wind vane on the left points in the direction the wind is blowing from. The anemometer on the right measures wind speed. The cups catch the wind, turning faster when the wind blows faster.

Local Winds

Have you ever flown a kite at the beach on a hot summer day? Even if there is no wind inland, there may be a cool breeze blowing in from the water toward the beach. This breeze is an example of a local wind. **Local winds** are winds that blow over short distances. **Local winds are caused by unequal heating of Earth's surface within a small area.** Local winds form only when no winds are blowing from farther away.

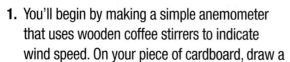

You and Your Community

WHERE'S THE WIND?

Your city is planning to build a new community center. You and your classmates want to be sure that the doors will not be hard to open or close on windy days. You need to know which side of the building will be sheltered from the wind. You decide to measure wind speeds around a similar building.

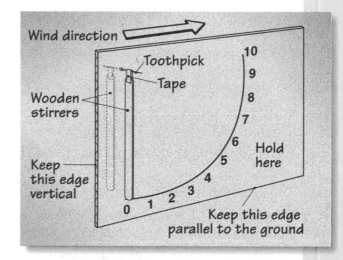

Problem

How can you determine wind patterns around a building?

Skills Focus

measuring, interpreting data, drawing conclusions

Materials

pen
wind vane
meter stick
corrugated cardboard sheet, 15 cm x 20 cm
round toothpick
2 wooden coffee stirrers
narrow masking tape

Procedure ✂

1. You'll begin by making a simple anemometer that uses wooden coffee stirrers to indicate wind speed. On your piece of cardboard, draw a curved scale like the one shown in the diagram. Mark it in equal intervals from 0 to 10.

2. Carefully use the pen to make a small hole where the toothpick will go. Insert the toothpick through the hole.

3. Tape the wooden coffee stirrers to the toothpick as shown in the diagram, one on each side of the cardboard.

4. Copy the data table into your notebook.

5. Take your anemometer outside the school. Stand about 2–3 m away from the building and away from any corners or large plants.

Unequal heating often occurs on land that is next to a large body of water. It takes more energy to warm up a body of water than it does to warm up an equal area of land. This means that as the sun heats Earth's surface during the day, the land warms up faster than the water. The air over the land becomes warmer than the air over the water. The warm air expands and rises, creating a low-pressure area. Cool air blows inland from the water and moves underneath the warm air. A wind that blows

DATA TABLE

Location	Wind Direction	Wind Speed

6. Use the wind vane to find out what direction the wind is coming from. Hold your anemometer so that the card is straight, vertical, and parallel to the wind direction. Observe which number the wooden stirrer is closest to. Record your data.
7. Repeat your measurements on all the other sides of the building. Record your data.

Analyze and Conclude

1. Was the wind stronger on one side of the school building than the other sides? How can you explain your observation?
2. Do your classmates' results agree with yours? What might account for any differences?
3. **Apply** Based on your data, which side of the building provides the best location for a door?

More to Explore

What effect do plants have on the wind speed in an area? Could bushes and trees be planted so that they reduce the wind speed near the doors? What measurements could you make to find out?

Warmer air rising

Cooler air moving to take warmer air's place

Warmer air rising

Cooler air moving to take warmer air's place

Figure 7 **A.** During the day, cool air moves from the sea to the land, creating a sea breeze. **B.** At night, cooler air moves from the land to the sea. *Forming Operational Definitions* *What type of breeze occurs at night?*

from an ocean or lake onto land is known as a **sea breeze** or a lake breeze. Figure 7A shows a sea breeze.

At night, the situation is reversed. Land cools more quickly than water, so the air over the land becomes cooler than the air over the water. As the warmer air over the water rises, cooler air moves from the land to take its place. The flow of air from land to a body of water is called a **land breeze.**

Monsoons

A process similar to land and sea breezes can occur over wider areas. In the summer in South and Southeast Asia, the land gradually gets warmer than the ocean. A large "sea breeze" blows steadily inland from the ocean all summer, even at night. In the winter, the land cools and becomes colder than the ocean. A "land breeze" blows steadily from the land to the ocean.

Sea and land breezes over a large region that change direction with the seasons are called **monsoons.** The summer monsoon in South Asia and Southeast Asia is very important for the crops grown there. The air blowing from the ocean during the rainy season is very warm and humid. As the humid air rises over the land, the air cools, producing heavy rains that supply the water needed by rice and other crops.

Figure 8 This heavy rain in Nepal is part of the summer monsoon, which blows from the ocean to the land. In the winter, the monsoon reverses and blows from the land to the ocean.

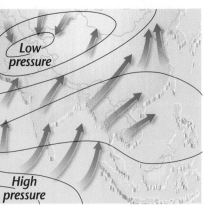

Summer Monsoon

Low pressure

High pressure

Winter Monsoon

High pressure

Low pressure

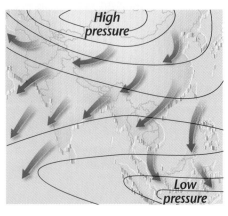

Global Winds

Winds that blow steadily from specific directions over long distances are called **global winds.** Like local winds, global winds are created by unequal heating of Earth's surface. Refer to Figure 9 to see how sunlight strikes Earth's surface. In the middle of the day near the equator, the sun is almost directly overhead. The direct rays from the sun heat Earth's surface intensely. Near the North Pole or South Pole, the sun's rays strike Earth's surface at a lower angle, even at noon. The sun's energy is spread out over a larger area, so it heats the surface less. As a result, temperatures near the poles are much lower than they are near the equator.

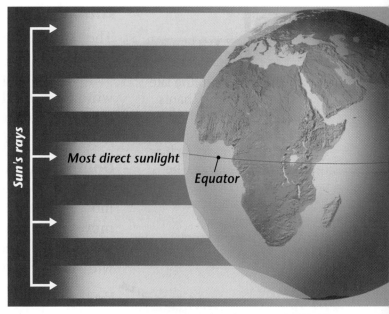

Most direct sunlight

Equator

Sun's rays

Figure 9 Near the equator, energy from the sun strikes Earth almost directly. Near the poles, the same amount of energy is spread out over a larger area.

Global Convection Currents Temperature differences between the equator and the poles produce giant convection currents in the atmosphere. Warm air rises at the equator, and cold air sinks at the poles. Therefore air pressure tends to be lower near the equator and greater near the poles, causing winds at Earth's surface to blow from the poles toward the equator. Higher in the atmosphere, air flows away from the equator toward the poles. **The movement of air between the equator and the poles produces global winds.**

The Coriolis Effect If Earth did not rotate, global winds would blow in a straight line from the poles toward the equator. Because Earth is rotating, global winds do not follow a straight path. As the winds move, Earth rotates from west to east underneath them, making it seem as if the winds have curved. The way Earth's rotation makes winds curve is called the **Coriolis effect** (kawr ee OH lis). It is named for the French mathematician who studied and explained it in 1835.

In the Northern Hemisphere, all global winds gradually turn toward the right. As you can see in Figure 10, a wind blowing toward the north gradually turns toward the northeast. In other words, a south wind gradually changes to a southwest wind. In the Southern Hemisphere, winds curve toward the left. A south wind becomes an southeast wind, and a north wind becomes a northwest wind.

Figure 10 As Earth rotates, the Coriolis effect turns winds in the Northern Hemisphere toward the right. *Interpreting Diagrams Which way do winds turn in the Southern Hemisphere?*

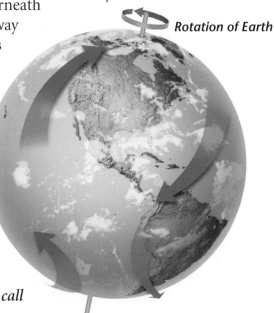

Rotation of Earth

Checkpoint What happens to a wind blowing toward the south in the Northern Hemisphere? What would you call this wind?

From colonial days to the late 1800s, American merchants traded new ships, lumber, cotton, tobacco, and furs for manufactured goods, such as textiles, from England. The eastbound voyage in the early 1800s took about three weeks. However, the westbound passage took almost twice as long—five to six weeks.

In Your Journal

Imagine that you are a sea captain making the voyage to England and back to America. Your family doesn't understand why your journey home takes almost twice as long as your journey to England. Write a letter to your family explaining why you have to travel farther south to take advantage of the prevailing winds on your return voyage.

Global Wind Belts

The Coriolis effect and other factors combine to produce a pattern of calm areas and wind belts around Earth. The calm areas include the doldrums and the horse latitudes. **The major global wind belts are the trade winds, the prevailing westerlies, and the polar easterlies.** As you read about each area, find it in *Exploring Global Winds*.

Doldrums Near the equator, the sun heats the surface strongly. Warm air rises steadily, creating an area of low pressure. Cool air moves into the area, but is warmed rapidly and rises before it moves very far. There is very little horizontal motion, so the winds near the equator are very weak. Regions near the equator with little or no wind are called the doldrums.

Horse Latitudes Warm air that rises at the equator divides and flows both north and south. **Latitude** is the distance from the equator, measured in degrees. At about 30° north and south latitudes, the air stops moving toward the poles and sinks. In each of these regions, another belt of calm air forms. Hundreds of years ago, sailors becalmed in these waters ran out of food and water for their horses and had to throw the horses overboard. Because of this, the latitudes 30° north and south of the equator are called the horse latitudes.

Trade Winds When the cold air over the horse latitudes sinks, it produces a region of high pressure. This high pressure causes surface winds to blow both toward the equator and away from it. The winds that blow toward the equator are turned west by the Coriolis effect. As a result, winds in the Northern Hemisphere between 30° north latitude and the equator blow generally from the northeast. In the Southern Hemisphere between 30° south latitude and the equator, the winds blow from the southeast. These steady easterly winds are called the trade winds. For hundreds of years, sailors relied on them to carry cargoes from Europe to the West Indies and South America.

Figure 11 The bark *Patriot*, built in 1809, carried goods to many parts of the world. *Applying Concepts How much effect do you think the prevailing winds have on shipping today?*

EXPLORING Global Winds

A series of wind belts circles Earth. Between the wind belts are calm areas where air is rising or falling.

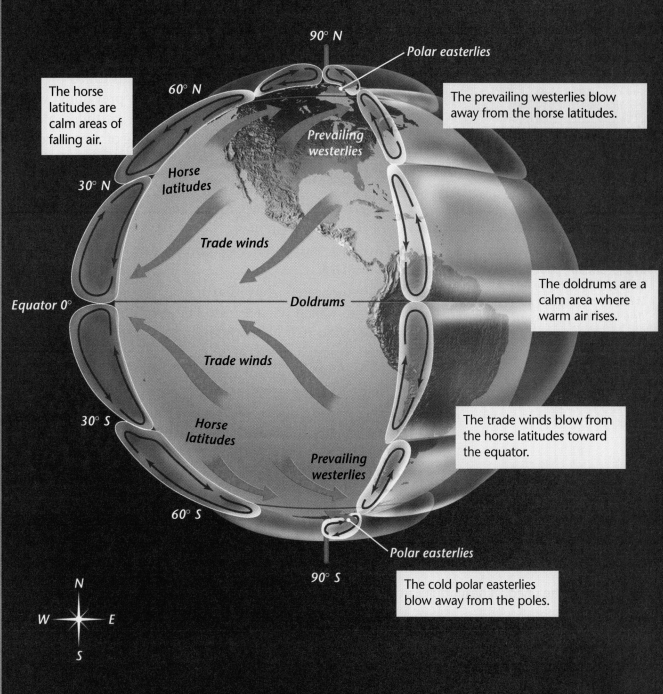

Polar easterlies

The horse latitudes are calm areas of falling air.

60° N

Prevailing westerlies

The prevailing westerlies blow away from the horse latitudes.

30° N

Horse latitudes

Trade winds

90° N

Equator 0°

Doldrums

The doldrums are a calm area where warm air rises.

Trade winds

30° S

Horse latitudes

Prevailing westerlies

The trade winds blow from the horse latitudes toward the equator.

60° S

Polar easterlies

90° S

The cold polar easterlies blow away from the poles.

N
W · E
S

Prevailing Westerlies In the mid-latitudes, winds that blow toward the poles are turned toward the east by the Coriolis effect. Because they blow from the west to the east, they are called prevailing westerlies. The prevailing westerlies blow generally from the southwest between 30° and 60° north latitudes and from the northwest between 30° and 60° south latitudes. The prevailing westerlies play an important part in the weather of the United States.

Polar Easterlies Cold air near the poles sinks and flows back toward lower latitudes. The Coriolis effect shifts these polar winds to the west, producing winds called the polar easterlies. The polar easterlies meet the prevailing westerlies at about 60° north and 60° south latitudes, along a region called the polar front. The mixing of warm and cold air along the polar front has a major effect on weather changes in the United States.

✓ *Checkpoint* **In what region do the polar easterlies meet the prevailing westerlies?**

Figure 12 By traveling east in a jet stream, pilots can save time and fuel. *Predicting What would happen if a plane flew west in a jet stream?*

Jet Streams

About 10 kilometers above Earth's surface are bands of high-speed winds called **jet streams.** These winds are hundreds of kilometers wide but only a few kilometers deep. Jet streams blow from west to east at speeds of 200 to 400 kilometers per hour. As jet streams travel around Earth, they wander north and south along a wavy path.

Airplanes are aided by a jet stream when traveling east. Pilots can save fuel and time by flying east in a jet stream. However, airplanes flying at jet stream altitudes are slowed down when traveling west against the jet stream winds.

Section 3 Review

1. How does the unequal heating of Earth's surface cause winds?
2. How are local winds and global winds similar? How are they different?
3. Name and draw the three major wind belts.
4. **Thinking Critically** **Applying Concepts** Imagine you are flying from Seattle to San Francisco, which is almost exactly due south of Seattle. Should the pilot set a course due south? Explain your answer.

Check Your Progress

CHAPTER PROJECT 2

Check with your teacher to be sure you are using the weather instruments correctly. Are you recording units for each measurement? Collect and record measurements each day.

SECTION
4 Water in the Atmosphere

DISCOVER ········· ·············· ACTIVITY

How Does Fog Form?

1. Fill a narrow-necked plastic bottle with hot tap water. Pour out most of the water, leaving about 3 cm at the bottom. **CAUTION:** *Avoid spilling hot water. Do not use water that is so hot that you cannot safely hold the bottle.*

2. Place an ice cube on the mouth of the bottle. What happens?

3. Repeat Steps 1 and 2 using cold water instead of hot water. What happens?

Think It Over
Developing Hypotheses How can you explain your observations? Why is there a difference between what happens with the hot water and with the cold water?

D
uring a rainstorm, the air feels moist. On a clear, cloudless day, the air may feel dry. As the sun heats the land and oceans, the amount of water in the atmosphere changes. Water is always moving between the atmosphere and Earth's surface.

This movement of water between the atmosphere and Earth's surface, called the water cycle, is shown in Figure 13. Water vapor enters the air by evaporation from the oceans and other bodies of water. **Evaporation** is the process by which water molecules in liquid water escape into the air as water vapor. Water vapor is also added to the air by living things. Water enters the roots of plants, rises to the leaves, and is released as water vapor.

As part of the water cycle, some of the water vapor in the atmosphere condenses to form clouds. Rain and other forms of precipitation fall from the clouds toward the surface. The water then runs off the surface, or moves through the ground, back into the oceans, lakes, and streams.

GUIDE FOR READING

◆ How is relative humidity measured?

◆ How do clouds form?

◆ What are the three main types of clouds?

Reading Tip Before you read, write a definition of "cloud." Revise your definition as you read about clouds.

The Water Cycle

Condensation

Precipitation

Evaporation from plants

Evaporation from oceans, lakes, and streams

Surface runoff

Figure 13 In the water cycle, water moves from lakes and oceans into the atmosphere and falls back to Earth.

Humidity

Humidity is a measure of the amount of water vapor in the air. The percentage of water vapor in the air compared to the maximum amount the air could hold is called the **relative humidity.** For example, at 10°C, 1 cubic meter of air can hold a maximum of 8 grams of water vapor. If there actually were 8 grams of water vapor in the air, then the relative humidity of the air would be 100 percent. If the air held 4 grams of water vapor, the relative humidity would be half, or 50 percent. The amount of water vapor that the air can hold depends on its temperature. Warm air can hold more water vapor than cool air.

INTEGRATING LIFE SCIENCE "It's not the heat, it's the humidity." What does this common expression mean? Even on a hot day, you can still feel comfortable if the air is dry. Evaporation of moisture from your skin removes heat and helps to keep your body's temperature comfortable. You feel less comfortable on a hot day if the relative humidity is high. When the relative humidity is high, evaporation slows down. Evaporation therefore has less cooling effect on your body.

Measuring Relative Humidity

Relative humidity can be measured with a psychrometer. A **psychrometer** (sy KRAHM uh tur) has two thermometers, a wet-bulb thermometer and a dry-bulb thermometer. The bulb of the wet-bulb thermometer has a cloth covering that is moistened with water. Air is then blown over both thermometers. Because the wet-bulb thermometer is cooled by evaporation, its reading drops below that of the dry-bulb thermometer.

Relative Humidity					
Dry-Bulb Reading (°C)	Difference Between Wet- and Dry-Bulb Readings (°C)				
	1	2	3	4	5
10	88	76	65	54	43
12	88	78	67	57	48
14	89	79	69	60	50
16	90	80	71	62	54
18	91	81	72	64	56
20	91	82	74	66	58
22	92	83	75	68	60
24	92	84	76	69	62
26	92	85	77	70	64
28	93	86	78	71	65
30	93	86	79	72	66

Figure 14 A sling psychrometer is used to measure relative humidity. First, find the wet-bulb and dry-bulb temperatures. Then find the dry-bulb temperature in the left column of the table. Find the difference between the wet- and dry-bulb temperatures across the top of the table. The number in the table where these two readings intersect indicates the relative humidity in percent.

If the relative humidity is high, the water on the wet bulb will evaporate slowly and the wet-bulb temperature will not change much. If the relative humidity is low, the water on the wet bulb will evaporate rapidly and the wet-bulb temperature will drop. The relative humidity can be found by comparing the temperatures of the wet-bulb and dry-bulb thermometers on a table like the one in Figure 14.

✓ *Checkpoint* **What is the difference between humidity and relative humidity?**

How Clouds Form

What do clouds remind you of? They can look like people, animals, countries, and a thousand other fanciful forms. Of course, not all clouds are fluffy and white. Storm clouds can be dark and cover the whole sky.

Clouds of all kinds form when water vapor in the air becomes liquid water or ice crystals. The process by which molecules of water vapor in the air become liquid water is called **condensation.** How does water condense? As you know, cold air can hold less water vapor than warm air. As air cools, the amount of water vapor it can hold decreases. Some of the water vapor in the air condenses to form droplets of liquid water.

The temperature at which condensation begins is called the **dew point.** If the dew point is below the freezing point, the water vapor may change directly into ice crystals. When you look at a cloud, you are seeing millions of tiny ice crystals or water droplets.

For water vapor to condense, tiny particles must be present so the water has a surface on which to condense. Most of these particles are salt crystals, dust from soil, and smoke. Sometimes water vapor condenses onto solid surfaces, such as blades of grass, instead of particles. Water that condenses from the air onto a cold surface is called dew. Frost is ice that has been deposited directly from the air onto a cold surface.

Clouds form whenever air is cooled to its dew point and particles are present. But why does the air cool? If air is warmed near the ground, it

Sharpen your Skills

Interpreting Data

ACTIVITY

At lunchtime you use a psychrometer and get readings of 26°C on the dry-bulb thermometer and 21°C on the wet-bulb thermometer. Use Figure 14 to find the relative humidity.

Later in the day you use the psychrometer again and this time get readings of 20°C on the dry-bulb thermometer and 19°C on the wet-bulb thermometer. Find the new relative humidity. Is the relative humidity increasing or decreasing?

Figure 15 Dew forms when water vapor condenses out of the air onto a solid surface, such as this flower.

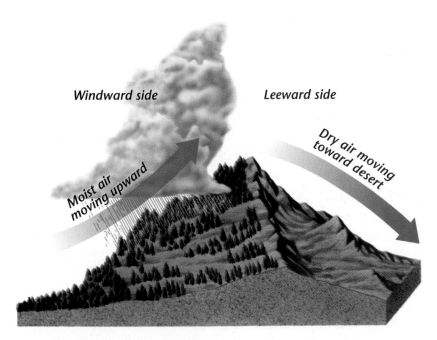

Windward side

Leeward side

Moist air moving upward

Dry air moving toward desert

Figure 16 Humid air cools as it is blown up the side of a mountain. *Predicting* What happens when water vapor condenses out of the air?

becomes less dense and rises in a convection current. When the rising air expands and becomes cooler, clouds may form.

When wind strikes the side of a hill or mountain, the air is forced upward. As the air rises along the slope, the air cools. Rain or snow falls on the windward side of the mountains, the side facing the on-coming wind.

By the time the air reaches the other side of the mountains, it has lost much of its water vapor. The air is cool and dry. The land on the leeward side of the mountains—downwind—is in a rain shadow. Just as very little light falls in a sun shadow, very little rain falls in a rain shadow. Not only has the air lost its water vapor while crossing the mountains, but the air has also grown warmer while flowing down the mountainside. This warm, dry air often creates a desert on the leeward side of the mountains.

☑ *Checkpoint* Why are the tops of some mountains almost always covered by clouds?

Types of Clouds

As you know, clouds come in different shapes. **Meteorologists classify clouds into three main types: cumulus, stratus, and cirrus.** Clouds are also classified by their altitude. Each type of cloud is associated with a different type of weather.

Clouds that look like fluffy, rounded piles of cotton are called **cumulus** (KYOO myuh lus) clouds. The word *cumulus* means "heap" or "mass." Cumulus clouds form less than 2 kilometers above the ground, but may grow in size and height until they extend upward as much as 18 kilometers. Cumulus clouds usually indicate fair weather. Towering clouds with flat tops, called cumulonimbus clouds, often produce thunderstorms. The suffix *-nimbus* comes from a Latin word meaning "rain."

Clouds that form in flat layers are called **stratus** (STRAT us) clouds. *Strato* means "spread out." Stratus clouds usually cover all or most of the sky. As stratus clouds thicken, they may produce drizzle, rain, or snow. They are then called nimbostratus clouds.

Wispy, feathery clouds are called **cirrus** (SEER us) clouds. Cirrus clouds form only at high levels, above about 6 kilometers, where temperatures are very low. As a result, cirrus clouds are made of ice crystals.

EXPLORING Clouds

The main types of clouds are cumulus, stratus, and cirrus. A cloud's name contains clues about its height and structure.

Cirrus

Cirrocumulus

Cirrus clouds
Cirrus, cirrostratus, and cirrocumulus clouds are made up of ice crystals.

Altocumulus

Cumulonimbus clouds
Thunderstorms come from cumulonimbus clouds. For this reason cumulonimbus clouds are also called thunderheads.

Altostratus

Cumulonimbus

Nimbostratus clouds
Nimbostratus clouds may produce rain or snow.

Nimbostratus

Cumulus clouds
Cumulus clouds are usually a sign of fair weather.

Stratus

Cumulus

Fog

Figure 17 Fog often forms at night over cool lakes. *Predicting What will happen as the sun rises and warms the air above the lake?*

Cirrus clouds that have feathery "hooked" ends are sometimes called mare's tails. Cirrocumulus clouds, which look like rows of cotton balls, often indicate that a storm is on its way.

Part of a cloud's name may be based on its height. The names of clouds that form between about 2 and 6 kilometers above Earth's surface have the prefix *alto-*, which means "high." The two main types of these clouds are altocumulus and altostratus.

Clouds that form at or near the ground are called fog. Fog often forms when the ground cools at night after a warm, humid day. The ground cools the air just above the ground to the air's dew point. The next day the heat of the morning sun "burns" the fog off as its water droplets evaporate.

Section 4 Review

1. What instrument is used to measure relative humidity? How does it work?
2. What conditions are needed for clouds to form?
3. Describe each of the three main types of clouds.
4. **Thinking Critically** **Classifying** Classify each of the following cloud types as low-level, medium-level, or high-level: altocumulus, altostratus, cirrostratus, cirrus, cumulus, fog, nimbostratus, and stratus.

Science at Home

Fill a large glass half-full with cold water. Show your family members what happens as you add ice cubes to the water. Explain to your family that the water that appears on the outside of the glass comes from water vapor in the atmosphere. Also explain why the water on the outside of the glass only appears after you add ice to the water in the glass.

SECTION 5 Precipitation

DISCOVER .... ACTIVITY

How Can You Make Hail?

1. Put on your goggles.
2. Put 15 g of salt into a beaker. Add 50 mL of water. Stir the solution until most of the salt is dissolved.
3. Put 15 mL of cold water in a clean test tube.
4. Place the test tube in the beaker.
5. Fill the beaker almost to the top with crushed ice. Stir the ice mixture every minute for six minutes.

6. Remove the test tube from the beaker and drop an ice chip into the test tube. What happens?

Think It Over

Inferring Based on your observation, what conditions are necessary for hail to form?

In Arica, Chile, the average rainfall is less than 1 millimeter per year. Many years pass with no precipitation at all. On the other hand, the average rainfall on Mount Waialeale on the island of Kauai in Hawaii is about 12 meters per year. That's more than enough to cover a three-story house! As you can see, rainfall varies greatly around the world.

Water evaporates into the air from every water surface on Earth and from living things. This water eventually returns to the surface as precipitation. **Precipitation** (pree sip uh TAY shun) is any form of water that falls from clouds and reaches Earth's surface.

Precipitation always comes from clouds. But not all clouds produce precipitation. For precipitation to occur, cloud droplets or ice crystals must grow heavy enough to fall through the air. One way that cloud droplets grow is by colliding and combining with other cloud droplets. As the droplets grow larger, they fall faster and collect more and more small droplets. Finally, the droplets become heavy enough to fall out of the cloud as raindrops.

Types of Precipitation

In warm parts of the world, precipitation is almost always rain or drizzle. In colder regions, precipitation may fall as snow or ice. **Common types of precipitation include rain, sleet, freezing rain, hail, and snow.**

GUIDE FOR READING

◆ What are the main types of precipitation?

◆ How is precipitation measured?

Reading Tip As you read, make a list of the types of precipitation. Write a sentence describing how each type forms.

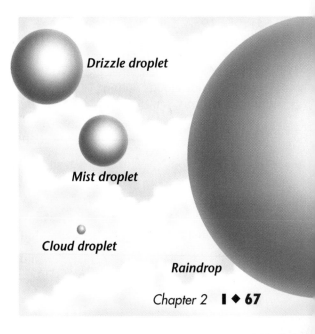

Drizzle droplet

Mist droplet

Cloud droplet

Raindrop

Figure 18 Droplets come in many sizes. Believe it or not, a raindrop has about one million times as much water in it as a cloud droplet.

Chapter 2 **I ◆ 67**

Figure 19 A. Snowflakes form in clouds that are colder than 0°C. B. Freezing rain coats objects with a layer of ice. C. Hailstones are formed inside clouds during thunderstorms.

Rain The most common kind of precipitation is rain. Drops of water are called rain if they are at least 0.5 millimeter in diameter. Precipitation made up of smaller drops of water is called mist or drizzle. Mist and drizzle usually fall from nimbostratus clouds.

Sleet Sometimes raindrops fall through a layer of air below 0°C, the freezing point of water. As they fall, the raindrops freeze into solid particles of ice. Ice particles smaller than 5 millimeters in diameter are called sleet.

Freezing Rain At other times raindrops falling through cold air near the ground do not freeze in the air. Instead, the raindrops freeze when they touch a cold surface. This is called freezing rain. In an ice storm, a smooth, thick layer of ice builds up on every surface. The weight of the ice may break tree branches onto power lines, causing power failures. Freezing rain and sleet can make sidewalks and roads slippery and dangerous.

Hail Round pellets of ice larger than 5 millimeters in diameter are called hailstones. Hail forms only inside cumulonimbus clouds during thunderstorms. A hailstone starts as an ice pellet inside a cold region of a cloud. Strong updrafts in the cloud carry the hailstone up and down through the cold region many times. Each time the hailstone goes through the cold region, a new layer of ice forms around the hailstone. Eventually the hailstone becomes heavy enough to fall to the ground. If you cut a hailstone in half, you can often see shells of ice, like the layers of an onion. Because hailstones can grow quite large before finally falling to the ground, hail can cause tremendous damage to crops, buildings, and vehicles.

Snow Often water vapor in a cloud is converted directly into ice crystals called snowflakes. Snowflakes have an endless number of different shapes and patterns, all with six sides or branches. Snowflakes often join together into larger clumps of snow in which the six-sided crystals are hard to see.

☑ *Checkpoint* *How do hailstones form?*

Measuring Precipitation

Meteorologists measure rainfall with a rain gauge. A rain gauge is an open-ended can or tube that collects rainfall. The amount of rainfall is measured by dipping a ruler into the water or by reading a marked scale. To increase the accuracy of the measurement, the top of a rain gauge may have a funnel that collects ten times as much rain as the tube alone. The funnel collects a greater depth of water that is easier to measure. But to get the actual depth of rain, it is necessary to divide by ten.

Snowfall is measured using a ruler or by melting collected snow and measuring the depth of water it produces. On average, 10 centimeters of snow contains about the same amount of water as 1 centimeter of rain. Of course, light, fluffy snow contains far less water than heavy, wet snow.

Collecting funnel

1 centimeter of rain

10 centimeters in measuring tube

Measuring tube $\frac{1}{10}$ area of funnel

Figure 20 A rain gauge measures the depth of rain that falls. *Observing How much rain was collected in the measuring tube of this rain gauge?*

Calculating

Make your own rain gauge by putting a funnel into a narrow, straight-sided glass jar. Here's how to calculate how much more rain your funnel collects than the jar alone.

ACTIVITY

1. First measure the diameter of the top of the funnel and square it.
   Example: 4 × 4 = 16
2. Then measure the diameter of the top of the jar and square it.
   Example: 2 × 2 = 4
3. Divide the first square by the second square.
   Example: $\frac{16}{4} = 4$
4. To find the actual depth of rain that fell, divide the depth of water in the jar by the ratio from Step 3.
   Example: $\frac{8 \text{ cm}}{4} = 2 \text{ cm}$

Controlling Precipitation

In some regions, there may be periods that are much drier than usual. Long periods of unusually low precipitation are called **droughts.** Droughts can cause great hardship. In the farming regions of the Midwest, for example, droughts may cause entire crops to fail. The farmers suffer from lost income and consumers suffer from high food prices. In some less-developed countries, droughts can cause widespread hunger, or famine.

INTEGRATING TECHNOLOGY In recent years, scientists have been trying to produce rain during droughts. The most common method is called cloud seeding. In cloud seeding, tiny crystals of dry ice (solid carbon dioxide) and silver iodide are sprinkled into clouds from airplanes. Many clouds contain supercooled water droplets, which are actually below 0°C. The droplets don't freeze because there aren't enough particles around which ice crystals can form. Water vapor can condense on the particles of silver iodide, forming rain or snow. Dry ice works by cooling the droplets even further, so that they will freeze without particles being present.

Cloud seeding has also been used with some success to clear fog from airports. Dry ice is sprinkled into the fog, causing ice crystals to form. This removes some of the fog so pilots can see the runways. Unfortunately, cloud seeding clears only cold fogs, so its use for this purpose is limited.

Figure 21 The corn in this photo was damaged by a long drought. *Applying Concepts How can cloud seeding be used to reduce the effect of droughts?*

Section 5 Review

1. Name the five common types of precipitation.
2. What device is used to measure precipitation?
3. What must happen before precipitation can fall from a cloud?
4. What kind of cloud produces hail?
5. **Thinking Critically Applying Concepts** If two open cans of different diameters were left out in the rain, how would the amount of water they collected compare? How would the depth of water in the cans compare?

Check Your Progress CHAPTER PROJECT 2
Now you should be ready to begin graphing your weather data. Look for patterns in your graphs. Use your data to predict what the next day's weather will be. Compare your predictions with what actually happens the next day. Are you able to predict the weather with confidence?

SECTION **1 Energy in the Atmosphere**

Key Ideas

◆ Energy from the sun travels to Earth as electromagnetic waves—mostly visible light, infrared radiation, and ultraviolet radiation.

◆ When Earth's surface is heated, it radiates some of the energy back into the atmosphere in the form of longer-wavelength radiation.

Key Terms

electromagnetic waves   ultraviolet radiation
radiation   scattering
infrared radiation   greenhouse effect

 SECTION **2 Heat Transfer**

INTEGRATING **PHYSICS**

Key Ideas

◆ The energy of motion in the molecules of a substance is called thermal energy.

◆ Three forms of heat transfer—radiation, conduction, and convection—work together to heat the troposphere.

Key Terms

thermal energy   thermometer   conduction
temperature   heat   convection

 SECTION **3 Winds**

Key Ideas

◆ All winds are caused by differences in air pressure, which are the result of unequal heating of Earth's surface.

◆ Local winds are caused by unequal heating of Earth's surface within a small area.

◆ The movement of air between the equator and the poles produces global winds.

Key Terms

wind   monsoon
anemometer   global wind
wind-chill factor   Coriolis effect
local wind   latitude
sea breeze   jet stream
land breeze

SECTION **4 Water in the Atmosphere**

Key Ideas

◆ Relative humidity is the percentage of water vapor in the air compared to the amount of water vapor the air could hold. It can be measured with a psychrometer.

◆ Clouds of all kinds form when water vapor in the air becomes liquid water or solid ice.

◆ Meteorologists classify clouds into three main types: cumulus, stratus, and cirrus.

Key Terms

evaporation   psychrometer   cumulus
humidity   condensation   stratus
relative humidity   dew point   cirrus

SECTION **5 Precipitation**

Key Ideas

◆ Common types of precipitation include rain, sleet, freezing rain, hail, and snow.

◆ Rain is measured with a rain gauge.

◆ Scientists have used cloud seeding to produce rain and to clear fog from airports.

Key Terms

precipitation
rain gauge
drought

Organizing Information

Concept Map Construct a concept map about winds on a separate sheet of paper. Be sure to include the following terms: local winds, global winds, monsoons, sea breezes, land breezes, prevailing westerlies, polar easterlies, tradewinds, and the two types of monsoon. (For more on concept maps, see the Skills Handbook.)

Reviewing Content

 For more review of key concepts, see the Interactive Student Tutorial CD-ROM.

Multiple Choice

Choose the letter of the best answer.

1. Energy from the sun travels to Earth's surface by
   a. radiation.
   b. convection.
   c. evaporation.
   d. conduction.
2. Rising warm air transports heat energy by
   a. conduction.
   b. convection.
   c. radiation.
   d. condensation.
3. A psychrometer is used to measure
   a. rainfall.
   b. relative humidity.
   c. temperature.
   d. humidity.
4. Clouds form because water vapor in the air
   a. warms.   b. conducts.
   c. condenses.   d. evaporates.
5. Rain, sleet, and hail are all forms of
   a. evaporation.
   b. condensation.
   c. precipitation.
   d. convection.

True or False

If the statement is true, write true. If it is false, change the underlined word or words to make the statement true.

6. Infrared radiation and <u>ultraviolet radiation</u> make up most of the energy Earth receives from the sun.
7. The process by which gases hold heat in the atmosphere is called the <u>wind-chill factor</u>.
8. Water molecules in liquid water escape into the atmosphere as water vapor in the process of <u>evaporation</u>.
9. The instrument used to measure wind speed is a <u>thermometer</u>.
10. Clouds that form near the ground are called <u>fog</u>.

Checking Concepts

11. What causes the greenhouse effect? How does it affect Earth's atmosphere?
12. What form of heat transfer is most important in heating the troposphere?
13. What are monsoons? How are they like land and sea breezes? How are they different?
14. Describe how the movements of hot air at the equator and cold air at the poles produce global wind patterns.
15. Why are deserts often found on the leeward side of mountain ranges?
16. Why do clouds usually form high in the air instead of near Earth's surface?
17. Describe sleet, hail, and snow in terms of how each one forms.
18. **Writing to Learn** Imagine you are a drop of water in the ocean. Write a diary describing your journey through the water cycle. How do you become a cloud? What type of conditions cause you to fall as precipitation? Use descriptive words to describe your journey.

Thinking Critically

19. **Relating Cause and Effect** What circumstances could cause a night-time land breeze in a city near the ocean?
20. **Problem Solving** If you use a psychrometer and get the same reading on both thermometers, what is the relative humidity?
21. **Comparing and Contrasting** How are hail and sleet alike? How are they different?
22. **Classifying** Classify the different types of clouds by the kind of weather associated with each type.
23. **Relating Cause and Effect** What is the source of the energy that powers Earth's winds?

Applying Skills

Use the table below to answer Questions 24–27.

Average Monthly Rainfall

Month	Rainfall	Month	Rainfall
January	1 cm	July	49 cm
February	1 cm	August	57 cm
March	1 cm	September	40 cm
April	2 cm	October	20 cm
May	25 cm	November	4 cm
June	52 cm	December	1 cm

24. **Graphing** Use the information in the table to draw a bar graph that shows the rainfall each month at this location.
25. **Calculating** What is the total amount of rainfall each year at this location?
26. **Classifying** Which months of the year would you classify as "dry"? Which months would you classify as "wet"?

27. **Drawing Conclusions** The place represented by the rainfall data is in Southeast Asia. What do you think accounts for the extremely heavy rainfall that occurs during some months?

CHAPTER PROJECT 2

Performance Assessment

Project Wrap Up Develop a way to present your findings to the class. For example, you could put your graphs and predictions on a poster. Are your graphs neatly drawn and easy to understand? Practice your presentation and make any needed improvements.

Reflect and Record How could you improve the accuracy of your observations? What did you learn about how easy or difficult it is to predict the weather?

Test Preparation
Use these questions to prepare for standardized tests.

Study the graph. Then answer Questions 28–31.

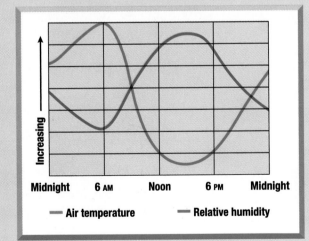

— Air temperature   — Relative humidity

28. The greatest change in air temperature occurred during the period from
    a. midnight to 6 A.M.
    b. 6 A.M. to noon.
    c. noon to 6 P.M.
    d. 6 P.M. to midnight.

29. The graph indicates that as air temperature increases, relative humidity
    a. increases.
    b. sometimes increases and sometimes decreases.
    c. decreases.
    d. stays about the same.

30. Condensation is most likely to occur at approximately
    a. 6 A.M.   b. noon.
    c. 3 P.M.   d. 6 P.M.

31. Assuming that the amount of water vapor in the air stayed constant through the day, one could infer from the graph that
    a. cool air can hold more water vapor than warm air.
    b. cool air can hold less water vapor than warm air.
    c. cool air and warm air can hold the same amount of water vapor.
    d. cool air cannot hold water vapor.

A lightning bolt tears
through the dark sky,
illuminating a field
of wheat.

www.phschool.com

PROJECT 3

The Weather Tomorrow

When the sky turns dark and threatening, it's not hard to predict the weather. A storm is on its way. But wouldn' you rather know about an approaching storm before it actually arrives?

In this chapter you will learn about weather patterns, including the kinds of patterns that cause strong thunderstorms like this one. As you work through this chapter, you will get a chance to make your own weather forecasts and compare them to the forecasts of professionals. Good luck!

Your Goal To predict the weather for your own community and two other locations in the United States.

To complete the project you will
- ◆ compare weather maps for several days at a time
- ◆ look for repeating patterns in the weather
- ◆ draw maps to show your weather predictions

Get Started Begin by previewing Section 4 to learn about weather maps and symbols. Start a project folder to hold daily national weather maps from your local newspaper and a description of the symbols used on the maps. Choose two locations in the United States that are at least 1,000 kilometers away from your community and from each other.

Check Your Progress You'll be working on this project as you study this chapter. To keep your project on track, look for Check Your Progress boxes at the following points.
> **Section 1 Review, page 82:** Collect weather maps and look for patterns.
> **Section 3 Review, page 98:** Predict the next day's weather.
> **Section 4 Review, page 105:** Compare your predictions to professional forecasts and to the actual weather.

Wrap Up At the end of the chapter (page 109), you will present your weather maps and discuss how well you predicted the weather.

SECTION 4 Predicting the Weather

Discover What's the Weather?
Sharpen Your Skills Interpreting Data
Skills Lab Reading a Weather Map

SECTION 1 Air Masses and Fronts

DISCOVER ••••••••••••••••••••••••••••••••••••ACTIVITY••••

How Do Fluids of Different Densities Behave?

1. Put on your apron. Place a cardboard divider across the middle of a plastic shoe box.

2. Add a few drops of red food coloring to a liter of warm water. Pour the red liquid, which represents low-density warm air, into the shoe box on one side of the divider.

3. Add about 100 mL of table salt and a few drops of blue food coloring to a liter of cold water. Pour the blue liquid, which represents high-density cold air, into the shoe box on the other side of the divider.

4. What do you think will happen if you remove the divider?

5. Now quickly remove the divider. Watch carefully from the side. What happens?

Think It Over

Developing Hypotheses Based on this activity, write a hypothesis stating what would happen if a mass of cold air ran into a mass of warm air.

GUIDE FOR READING

◆ What are the major types of air masses that affect the weather in North America?

◆ What are the main types of fronts?

◆ What are cyclones and anticyclones?

Reading Tip Before you read, use the headings to make an outline about air masses and fronts. Leave space to fill in details as you read.

Listen to the evening news and you may hear a weather forecast like this: "A huge mass of Arctic air is moving our way, bringing freezing temperatures." Today's weather is influenced by air from thousands of kilometers away—perhaps from Canada or the Caribbean Sea. A huge body of air that has similar temperature, humidity, and air pressure throughout it is called an **air mass.** A single air mass may spread over an area of millions of square kilometers and be up to 10 kilometers high.

Types of Air Masses

Scientists classify air masses according to two characteristics: temperature and humidity. Whether an air mass is warm or cold depends on the temperature of the region over which the air mass forms. **Tropical,** or warm, air masses form in the tropics and have low air pressure. **Polar,** or cold, air masses form north of 50° north latitude and south of 50° south latitude. Polar air masses have high air pressure.

Whether an air mass is humid or dry depends on whether it forms over water or land. **Maritime** air masses form over oceans. Water evaporates from the oceans, so the air can become very humid. **Continental** air masses form over land, in the middle of continents, and are dry.

Today

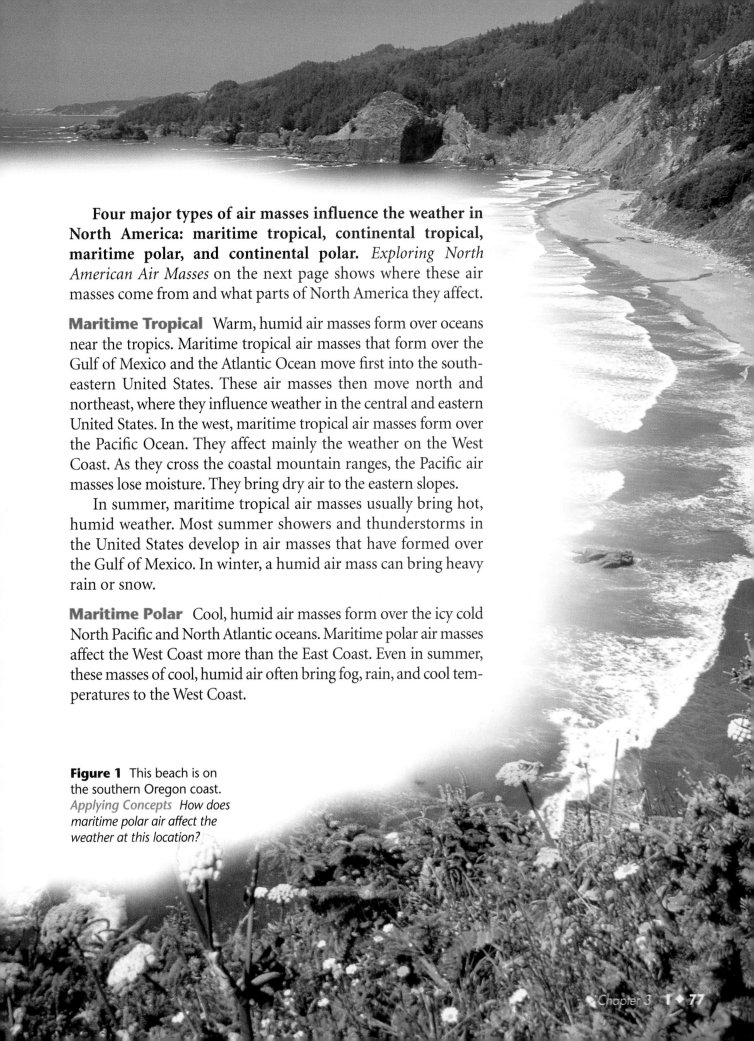

Four major types of air masses influence the weather in North America: maritime tropical, continental tropical, maritime polar, and continental polar. *Exploring North American Air Masses* on the next page shows where these air masses come from and what parts of North America they affect.

Maritime Tropical Warm, humid air masses form over oceans near the tropics. Maritime tropical air masses that form over the Gulf of Mexico and the Atlantic Ocean move first into the southeastern United States. These air masses then move north and northeast, where they influence weather in the central and eastern United States. In the west, maritime tropical air masses form over the Pacific Ocean. They affect mainly the weather on the West Coast. As they cross the coastal mountain ranges, the Pacific air masses lose moisture. They bring dry air to the eastern slopes.

In summer, maritime tropical air masses usually bring hot, humid weather. Most summer showers and thunderstorms in the United States develop in air masses that have formed over the Gulf of Mexico. In winter, a humid air mass can bring heavy rain or snow.

Maritime Polar Cool, humid air masses form over the icy cold North Pacific and North Atlantic oceans. Maritime polar air masses affect the West Coast more than the East Coast. Even in summer, these masses of cool, humid air often bring fog, rain, and cool temperatures to the West Coast.

Figure 1 This beach is on the southern Oregon coast. *Applying Concepts How does maritime polar air affect the weather at this location?*

EXPLORING North American Air Masses

A ir masses can be warm or cold, and humid or dry. As an air mass moves into an area, it changes the weather there.

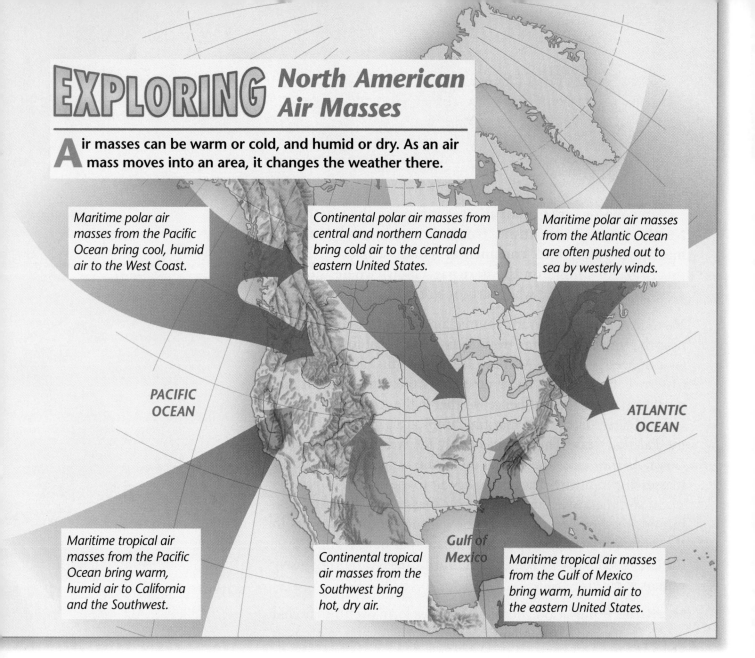

Maritime polar air masses from the Pacific Ocean bring cool, humid air to the West Coast.

Continental polar air masses from central and northern Canada bring cold air to the central and eastern United States.

Maritime polar air masses from the Atlantic Ocean are often pushed out to sea by westerly winds.

PACIFIC OCEAN

ATLANTIC OCEAN

Maritime tropical air masses from the Pacific Ocean bring warm, humid air to California and the Southwest.

Continental tropical air masses from the Southwest bring hot, dry air.

Gulf of Mexico

Maritime tropical air masses from the Gulf of Mexico bring warm, humid air to the eastern United States.

Continental Tropical Hot, dry air masses form only in summer over dry areas of the Southwest and northern Mexico. Continental tropical air masses cover a smaller area than other air masses. They occasionally move northeast, bringing hot, dry weather to the southern Great Plains.

Continental Polar Large continental polar air masses form over central and northern Canada and Alaska. As you would expect, continental polar air masses bring cool or cold air. In winter, continental polar air masses bring clear, cold, dry air to much of North America. Air masses that form near the Arctic Circle can bring bitterly cold weather with very low humidity. In summer, storms may occur when continental polar air masses move south and meet maritime tropical air masses moving north.

☑ *Checkpoint* *Where do continental polar air masses come from?*

How Air Masses Move

Recall that the prevailing westerlies are the major wind belts in the continental United States. The prevailing westerlies generally push air masses from west to east. For example, maritime polar air masses from the Pacific Ocean are blown onto the West Coast, bringing heavy rain or snow. Continental polar air masses from central Canada enter the United States between the Rocky Mountains and the Great Lakes. These cold, dry air masses are then blown east, where they affect the weather of the central and eastern United States.

Fronts

As huge masses of air move across the land and the oceans, they bump into each other. But the air masses do not easily mix. Why don't they? Think about a bottle of oil-and-vinegar salad dressing. The less dense oil floats on top of the more dense vinegar.

Something similar happens when two air masses with different temperatures and densities collide. The area where the air masses meet and do not mix becomes a **front.** The term *front,* which is borrowed from military language, means a battle area where opposing armies meet to fight. When air masses meet at a front, the collision often causes storms and changeable weather. A front may be 15 to 200 kilometers wide and extend as much as 10 kilometers up into the troposphere.

There are four types of fronts: cold fronts, warm fronts, stationary fronts, and occluded fronts. The kind of front that develops depends on the characteristics of the air masses and how they are moving. How does each type of front affect your local weather?

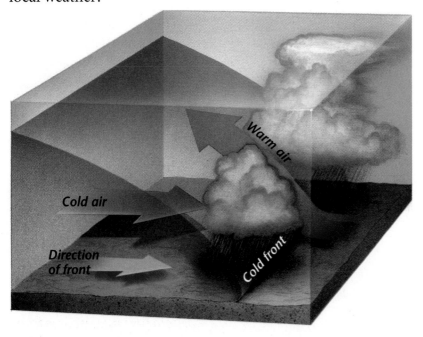

Figure 2 A cold front forms when cold air moves underneath warm air, forcing the warm air to rise.

Cold Fronts As you know, cold air is dense and tends to sink. Warm air is less dense and tends to rise. When a rapidly moving cold air mass runs into a slowly moving warm air mass, the denser cold air slides under the lighter warm air. The warm air is pushed upward, as shown in Figure 2. The front that forms is called a cold front.

As the warm air rises, it cools. Remember that warm air can hold more water vapor than cool air. The rising air soon reaches the dew point, the temperature at which the water vapor in the air condenses into droplets of liquid water. Clouds form. If there is a lot of water vapor in the warm air, heavy rain or snow may fall. What will happen if the warm air mass contains only a little water vapor? In this case, the cold front may be accompanied by only cloudy skies.

Cold fronts move quickly, so they can cause abrupt weather changes, including violent thunderstorms. After a cold front passes through an area, cool, dry air moves in, often bringing clear skies and cooler temperatures.

Warm Fronts Clouds, storms, and rain also accompany warm fronts. At a warm front, a moving warm air mass collides with a slowly moving cold air mass. Because cold air is more dense than warm air, the warm air moves over the cold air, as shown in Figure 3. If the warm air is humid, showers and light rain fall along the front where the warm and cold air meet. If the warm air is dry, scattered clouds form. Because warm fronts move more slowly than cold fronts, the weather may be rainy or foggy for several days. After a warm front passes through an area, the weather is likely to be warm and humid. In winter, warm fronts bring snow.

Figure 3 A warm front forms when warm air moves over cold air.
Interpreting Diagrams
What kind of weather forms at a warm front?

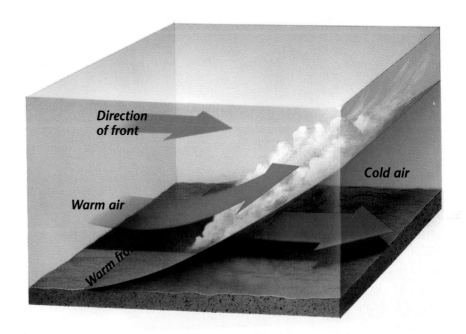

Direction of front

Warm air

Cold air

Warm fro

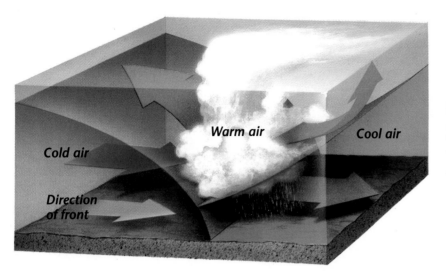

Figure 4 When a cold air mass and a cool air mass come together, the warm air caught between them is forced upward. The result is an occluded front.

Stationary Fronts Sometimes cold and warm air masses meet, but neither one has enough force to move the other. The two air masses face each other in a "standoff." In this case, the front is called a stationary front. Where the warm and cool air meet, water vapor in the warm air condenses into rain, snow, fog, or clouds. If a stationary front remains stalled over an area, it may bring many days of clouds and precipitation.

Occluded Fronts The most complex weather situation occurs at an occluded front, shown in Figure 4. At an occluded front, a warm air mass is caught between two cooler air masses. The denser cool air masses move underneath the less dense warm air mass and push it upward. The two cooler air masses meet in the middle and may mix. The temperature near the ground becomes cooler. The warm air mass is cut off, or **occluded,** from the ground. As the warm air cools and its water vapor condenses, the weather may turn cloudy and rainy or snowy.

☑ *Checkpoint* *What type of front forms when two air masses meet and neither one can move?*

Cyclones and Anticyclones

If you look at a weather map, you will see areas marked with an L. The L is short for "low," and indicates an area of relatively low air pressure. A swirling center of low air pressure is called a **cyclone,** from a Greek word meaning "wheel."

As warm air at the center of a cyclone rises, the air pressure decreases. Cooler air blows toward this low-pressure area from nearby areas where the air pressure is higher. Winds spiral inward toward the center of the system. Recall that in the Northern Hemisphere the Coriolis effect deflects winds to the right.

Classifying

At home, watch the weather forecast on television. Make a note of each time the weather reporter mentions a front. Classify the fronts mentioned or shown as cold, warm, stationary, or occluded. Also, note what type of weather is predicted to occur when the front arrives. Is each type of front always associated with the same type of weather?

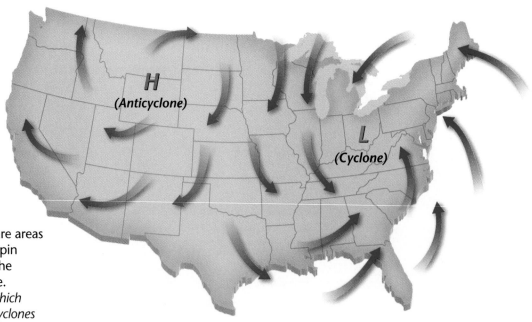

Figure 5 Cyclones are areas of low pressure that spin counterclockwise in the Northern Hemisphere. *Interpreting Maps Which way do winds in anticyclones spin?*

Because of this, winds in a cyclone spin counterclockwise in the Northern Hemisphere, as shown in Figure 5.

Cyclones play a large part in the weather of the United States. As air rises in a cyclone, the air cools, forming clouds and precipitation. **Cyclones and decreasing air pressure are associated with storms and precipitation.**

As its name suggests, an anticyclone is the opposite of a cyclone in most ways. **Anticyclones** are high-pressure centers of dry air. Anticyclones are also called "highs"—H on a weather map. Winds spiral outward from the center of an anticyclone, moving toward areas of lower pressure. Because of the Coriolis effect, winds in an anticyclone spin clockwise in the Northern Hemisphere. Because air moves out from the center of the anticyclone, cool air moves downward from higher in the troposphere. As the cool air falls, it warms up, so its relative humidity drops. The descending air in an anticyclone causes dry, clear weather.

Section 1 Review

1. What two main characteristics are used to classify air masses?
2. What is a front? Name and describe four types of fronts.
3. What is a cyclone? What type of weather does it bring?
4. Why do maritime polar air masses have more effect on the West Coast than the East Coast?
5. **Thinking Critically** **Classifying** Classify the four major types of air masses according to whether they are dry or humid.

Check Your Progress

CHAPTER PROJECT 3

Collect newspaper weather maps for about a week, and arrange them in order. Look carefully at how symbols on the map have moved from one day to the next. What patterns do you see from day to day in different weather factors? How does the weather in your community differ from the weather in the two other locations you selected?

SECTION 2 Storms

DISCOVER · ACTIVITY · · ·

Can You Make a Tornado?

1. Fill a large jar three-quarters full with water. Add a drop of liquid dish detergent and a penny or marble.

2. Put the lid on the jar tightly. Now move the jar in a circle until the water inside begins to spin.

Think It Over

Observing What happens to the water in the jar? Describe the pattern that forms. How is it like a tornado? Unlike a tornado?

Early in 1998, a series of powerful tornadoes roared through central Florida. With winds as high as 210 miles per hour, the tornadoes dropped cars into living rooms, crumpled trailers, and destroyed businesses and school buildings. They were the deadliest tornadoes ever to hit Florida. These tornadoes were not the only violent weather that year. In California the problem was rain. Record rainfalls brought devastating floods and mudslides.

What was causing these disasters? Meteorologists had an answer: El Niño. El Niño is a weather pattern related to the temperature of the water in the tropical Pacific Ocean. When temperatures there rise, they set off a series of events that can influence weather half a world away.

Have you ever experienced a tornado, hurricane, or other severe storm? When rain pours down, thunder crashes, or snowdrifts pile up, it may be hard to think about the actions of air pressure and air masses. Yet these are the causes of severe storms as well as the weather you experience every day.

A **storm** is a violent disturbance in the atmosphere. Storms involve sudden changes in air pressure, which in turn cause rapid air movements. Conditions that bring one kind of storm often cause other kinds of storms in the same area. For example, the conditions that cause thunderstorms can also cause tornadoes.

GUIDE FOR READING

◆ What are the main kinds of storms? How do they form?

◆ What measures can you take to ensure safety in a storm?

Reading Tip As you read, create a table comparing thunderstorms, tornadoes, hurricanes, and snowstorms. Include temperature, precipitation, and safety rules.

Figure 6 Tornadoes caused tremendous damage in Florida and other parts of the southeastern United States in 1998.

Figure 7 The anvil shape of this cloud is typical of cumulonimbus clouds that produce thunderstorms. *Applying Concepts Why do cumulonimbus clouds often form along cold fronts?*

Lightning Distances

Because light travels faster than sound, you see a lightning flash before you hear the clap of thunder. Here's how to calculate your distance from a thunderstorm.

CAUTION: *Do this activity inside a building only.*

1. Count the number of seconds between the moment when you see the lightning and when you hear the thunder.

2. Divide the number of seconds you counted by three to get the distance in kilometers. Example:

$$\frac{15 \text{ s}}{3 \text{ s/km}} = 5 \text{ km}$$

Calculating Wait for another flash of lightning and calculate the distance again. How can you tell whether a thunderstorm is moving toward you or away from you?

Thunderstorms

Do you find thunderstorms frightening? Exciting? A little of both? As you watch the brilliant flashes of lightning and listen to long rolls of thunder, you have probably wondered what caused them.

How Thunderstorms Form Thunderstorms are heavy rainstorms accompanied by thunder and lightning. **Thunderstorms form within large cumulonimbus clouds, or thunderheads.** Most cumulonimbus clouds and thunderstorms form when warm air is forced upward at a cold front. Cumulonimbus clouds also form on hot, humid afternoons in the spring and summer. In both cases, the warm, humid air rises rapidly. As the air rises, it cools, forming dense thunderheads. Heavy rain falls, sometimes along with hail.

Thunderstorms produce strong upward and downward winds—updrafts and downdrafts—inside clouds. When a downdraft strikes the ground, the air spreads out in all directions, producing bursts of wind called wind shear. Wind shear has caused a number of airplane accidents during takeoff or landing.

Lightning and Thunder During a thunderstorm, areas of positive and negative electrical charges build up in the storm clouds. **Lightning** is a sudden spark, or energy discharge, as these charges jump between parts of a cloud, between nearby clouds, or between a cloud and the ground. Lightning is similar to the shocks you sometimes feel when you touch a metal object on a very dry day, but on a much larger scale.

What causes thunder? A lightning bolt can heat the air near it to as much as 30,000°C, much hotter than the surface of the sun. The rapidly heated air expands suddenly and explosively. Thunder is the sound of the explosion. Because light travels faster than sound, you see lightning before you hear thunder.

Thunderstorm Safety When lightning strikes
 the ground, the hot, expanding air can shatter tree trunks or start forest fires. When lightning strikes people or animals, it acts like a powerful electric shock. Being struck by lightning can cause unconsciousness, serious burns, or even heart failure.

What should you do to remain safe if you are caught outside during a thunderstorm? **During thunderstorms, avoid touching metal objects because they can conduct electricity from lightning into your body.** Lightning usually strikes the tallest nearby object, such as a tree, house, or flagpole. To protect buildings from lightning, people install metal lightning rods at the highest point on a roof. Lightning rods intercept a lightning stroke and conduct the electricity through cables safely into the ground.

In open spaces, such as a golf course, people can be in danger because they are the tallest objects in the area. It is equally dangerous to seek shelter under a tree, because lightning may strike the tree and you at the same time. Instead, find a low area away from trees, fences, and poles. Crouch with your head down and your hands on your knees. If you are swimming or in a boat, get to shore and find shelter away from the water.

If you are inside a house during a thunderstorm, avoid touching telephones, electrical appliances, or plumbing fixtures, all of which can conduct electricity into the house. It is usually safe to stay in a car with a hard top during a thunderstorm because the electricity will move along the metal skin of the car and jump to the ground. However, do not touch any metal inside the car.

☑ *Checkpoint* *Why is lightning dangerous?*

Figure 8 Lightning occurs when electricity jumps within clouds, between clouds, or between a cloud and the ground.

Tornadoes

A tornado is one of the most frightening and destructive types of storms. A **tornado** is a rapidly whirling, funnel-shaped cloud that reaches down from a storm cloud to touch Earth's surface. If a tornado occurs over a lake or ocean, it is known as a waterspout. Tornadoes are usually brief, but can be deadly. They may touch the ground for 15 minutes or less and be only a few hundred meters across, but wind speeds may approach 480 kilometers per hour.

How Tornadoes Form **Tornadoes develop in low, heavy cumulonimbus clouds—the same clouds that bring thunderstorms.** Tornadoes are most likely to occur when thunderstorms are likely—in spring and early summer, often late in the afternoon when the ground is warm. The Great Plains often have the kind of weather pattern that is likely to create tornadoes: a warm, humid air mass moves north from the Gulf of Mexico into the lower Great Plains. A cold, dry air mass moves south from Canada. When the air masses meet, the cold air moves under the warm air, which rises. A squall line of thunderstorms is likely to form, with storms traveling from southwest to northeast. A single squall line can cause 10 or more tornadoes.

Tornadoes occur more often in the United States than in any other country. About 800 tornadoes occur in the United States

Weather That Changed History

Unanticipated storms have caused incredible damage, killed numbers of people, and even changed the course of history.

1281 Japan

In an attempt to conquer Japan, Kublai Khan, the Mongol emperor of China, sent a fleet of ships carrying a huge army. A hurricane from the Pacific brought high winds and towering waves that sank the ships. The Japanese named the storm *kamikaze,* meaning "divine wind."

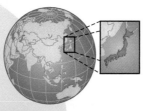

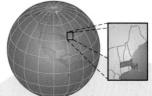

1620 Massachusetts

English Pilgrims set sail for the Americas in the *Mayflower.* They had planned to land near the mouth of the Hudson River, but turned back north because of rough seas and storms. When the Pilgrims landed farther north, they decided to stay and so established Plymouth Colony.

| 1300 | 1400 | 1500 | 1600 |

1588 England

King Philip II of Spain sent the Spanish Armada, a fleet of 130 ships, to invade England. Strong winds in the English Channel trapped the Armada near shore. Some Spanish ships escaped, but storms wrecked most of them.

86 ◆ I

every year. Weather patterns on the Great Plains result in a "tornado alley," shown in Figure 9, that runs from north-central Texas across central Oklahoma, Kansas, and Nebraska. However, tornadoes can and do occur in nearly every part of the United States.

☑ *Checkpoint* *Where do tornadoes form?*

Tornado Safety A tornado can level houses on one street, but leave neighboring houses standing. Tornado damage comes from both strong winds and flying debris. The low pressure inside the tornado sucks up dust and other objects into the funnel. Tornadoes can move large objects—sheds, trailers, cars—and scatter debris many miles away. One tornado tore off a motel sign in Broken Bow, Oklahoma, and dropped it 30 miles away in Arkansas!

INTEGRATING HEALTH

In Your Journal

Some of these events happened before forecasters had the equipment to predict weather scientifically. Choose one of the events in the time line. Write a paragraph describing how history might have been different if the people involved had had accurate weather predictions.

1870 Great Lakes

Learning that more than 1,900 boats had sunk in storms on the Great Lakes in 1869, Congress decided to set up a national weather service, the Army Signal Corps. In 1891 the job of issuing weather warnings and forecasts went to a new agency, the U.S. Weather Bureau.

1700   **1800**   **1900**

1837 North Carolina

The steamship *Home* sank during a hurricane off Ocracoke, North Carolina. In one of the worst storm-caused disasters at sea, 90 people died. In response, the U.S. Congress passed a law requiring seagoing ships to carry a life preserver for every passenger.

1915 Texas

When a hurricane struck the port city of Galveston in 1900, it killed 6,000 people and destroyed much of the city. As a result, a seawall 5 meters high and 16 kilometers long was built. When another hurricane struck in 1915, the seawall greatly reduced the amount of damage.

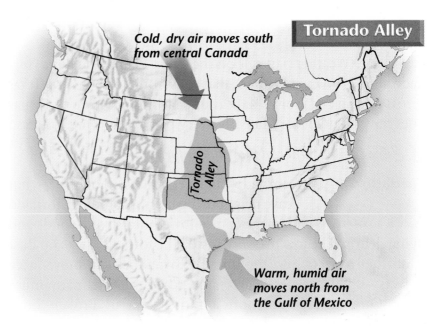

Cold, dry air moves south from central Canada

Tornado Alley

Tornado Alley

Warm, humid air moves north from the Gulf of Mexico

Figure 9 A tornado can cause a lot of damage in a short period of time. The map shows where tornadoes are most likely to occur in the United States.
Interpreting Maps Which states are partially located in "tornado alley"?

What should you do if a tornado is predicted in your area? A "tornado watch" is an announcement that tornadoes are possible in your area. Watch for approaching thunderstorms. A "tornado warning" is an announcement that a tornado has been seen in the sky or on weather radar. If you hear a tornado warning, move to a safe area as soon as you can. Do not wait until you actually see the tornado.

The safest place to be during a tornado is in the basement of a well-built building. If the building you are in does not have a basement, move to the middle of the ground floor. Stay away from windows and doors that could break and fly through the air. Lie on the floor under a sturdy piece of furniture, such as a large table. If you are outdoors or in a car or mobile home, move to a building or lie flat in a ditch.

✓ *Checkpoint What is the difference between a tornado watch and a tornado warning?*

Hurricanes

Between June and November, people who live in the eastern United States hear weather reports much like this: "A hurricane warning has been issued for the Atlantic coast from Florida to North Carolina. Hurricane Michael has winds of over 160 kilometers per hour and is moving north at about 65 kilometers per hour." A **hurricane** is a tropical storm that has winds of 119 kilometers per hour or higher. A typical hurricane is about 600 kilometers across.

Hurricanes also form in the Pacific and Indian oceans. In the western Pacific Ocean, hurricanes are called typhoons. Although hurricanes may be destructive, they bring much-needed rainfall to South Asia and Southeast Asia.

How Hurricanes Form A typical hurricane that strikes the United States forms in the Atlantic Ocean north of the equator in August, September, or October. **A hurricane begins over warm water as a low-pressure area, or tropical disturbance.** If the tropical disturbance grows in size and strength, it becomes a tropical storm, which may then become a hurricane.

A hurricane gets its energy from the warm, humid air at the ocean's surface. As this air rises and forms clouds, more air is drawn into the system. As with other storm systems, winds spiral inward toward the areas of low pressure. Inside the storm are bands of very high winds and heavy rains. The lowest air pressure and warmest temperatures are at the center of the hurricane. The lower the air pressure at the center of a storm, the faster the winds blow toward the center. Hurricane winds may be as strong as 320 kilometers per hour.

The Eye of the Hurricane The center of a hurricane is a ring of clouds surrounding a quiet "eye," as shown in Figure 10. If you were in the path of a hurricane, you would notice that the wind gets stronger as the eye approaches. When the eye arrives, the weather changes suddenly. The winds grow calm and the sky may clear. After the eye passes, the storm resumes, but the wind blows from the opposite direction.

How Hurricanes Move Hurricanes last longer than other storms, usually a week or more. Hurricanes that form in the Atlantic Ocean are steered by easterly trade winds toward the Caribbean islands and the southeastern United States. After a hurricane passes over land, it no longer has warm, moist air to draw energy from. The hurricane gradually slows down and loses strength, although heavy rainfall may continue for a number of days.

Figure 10 In a hurricane, air moves rapidly around a low-pressure area called the eye. *Observing* *Where is the eye of the hurricane in the photograph?*

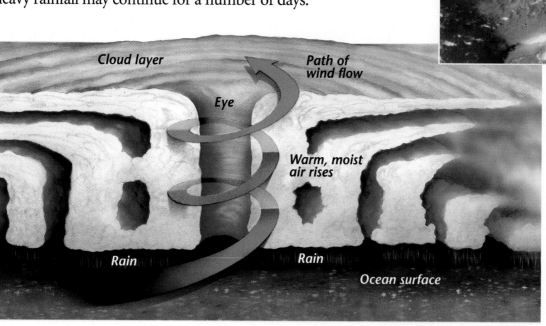

Cloud layer

Path of wind flow

Eye

Warm, moist air rises

Rain

Rain

Ocean surface

Visual Arts
CONNECTION

Weather and storms are favorite subjects for artists. "Snow Storm" is an oil painting by English artist J.M.W. Turner (1775–1851). To convey a mood or feeling, artists choose certain colors and textures. How does Turner's choice of colors enhance the mood of the painting? What texture do you see in the sea and sky? How does the texture support the feeling of the painting?

In Your Journal

Write a paragraph or two about the mood of this painting. Describe how you would feel being out in the wind and waves. Before you begin writing, jot down words that describe what you would see, hear, touch, taste, and smell. Exchange your descriptive writing with a partner to get feedback.

Hurricane Damage When a hurricane comes ashore, it brings high waves and severe flooding as well as wind damage. Hurricanes uproot trees, smash buildings, and destroy power lines. Heavy rains flood roads.

One of the most dangerous features of a hurricane is the storm surge. The low pressure and high winds of the hurricane over the ocean raise the level of the water up to six meters above normal sea level. The result is a **storm surge,** a "dome" of water that sweeps across the coast where the hurricane lands. As the hurricane comes onshore, the water comes with it. Storm surges can cause great damage, washing away beaches and destroying buildings along the coast.

Hurricane Safety Until the 1950s, a fast-moving hurricane *INTEGRATING HEALTH* could strike with little warning. Since then, advances in communications and satellite tracking have made hurricanes less deadly. People now receive information well in advance of an approaching hurricane.

A "hurricane watch" is an announcement that hurricane conditions are *possible* in your area within the next 36 hours. People should be prepared to **evacuate** (ee VAK yoo ayt), or move away temporarily.

A "hurricane warning" means that hurricane conditions are *expected* within 24 hours. **If you hear a hurricane warning and are told to evacuate, leave the area immediately.** If you must stay in a house, move to the interior of the building, away from windows.

☑ *Checkpoint* What is a storm surge?

Winter Storms

In the winter in the northern United States, much precipitation falls as snow. **Snow falls when humid air cools below 0°C.** Heavy snowfalls can block roads, trapping people in their homes and making it hard for emergency vehicles to move. Extreme cold can damage crops and cause water pipes to freeze and burst.

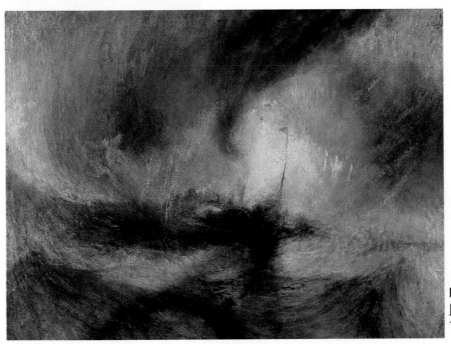

Figure 11 The British artist J.M.W. Turner painted "Snow Storm" in 1842.

Lake-effect Snow Two of the snowiest cities in the United States are Buffalo and Rochester in upstate New York. On average, nearly three meters of snow falls on each of these cities every winter. Why do Buffalo and Rochester get so much snow?

Study Figure 12. Notice that Buffalo is located to the east of Lake Erie, and Rochester is located to the south of Lake Ontario. In the fall and winter, the land near these lakes cools much more rapidly than the water in the lakes. Although the water in these lakes is cold, it is still much warmer than the surrounding land and air. When a cold, dry air mass moves from central Canada southeast across one of the Great Lakes, it picks up water vapor and heat from the lake. As soon as the air mass reaches the other side of the lake, the air rises and cools again. The water vapor condenses and falls as snow, usually within 40 kilometers of the lake.

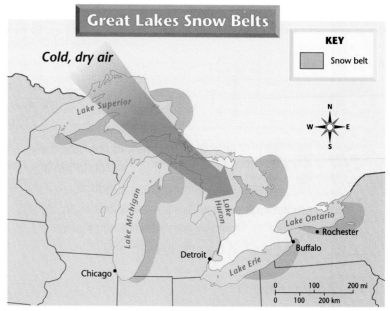

Figure 12 As cold dry air moves across the warmer water, it picks up water vapor. When the air reaches land and cools, lake-effect snow falls. *Interpreting Maps* Which two cities receive large amounts of snow?

Snowstorm Safety Imagine being out in a snowstorm when

![Integrating Health] **INTEGRATING HEALTH** the wind suddenly picks up. High winds can blow falling snow sideways or pick up snow from the ground and suspend it in the air. This situation can be extremely dangerous because the blowing snow makes it easy to get lost. Also, strong winds cool a person's body rapidly. **If you are caught in a snowstorm, try to find shelter from the wind.** Cover exposed parts of your body and try to stay dry. If you are in a car, the driver should keep the engine running only if the exhaust pipe is clear of snow.

Section 2 Review

1. What weather conditions are most likely to cause thunderstorms and tornadoes?
2. What is the most common path for the hurricanes that strike the United States?
3. What safety precautions should you take if a tornado is predicted in your area? If a hurricane is predicted?
4. **Thinking Critically** **Applying Concepts** In the winter, cool, humid air from the Pacific Ocean blows across the cold land of southern Alaska. What kind of storm do you think this causes?

Science at Home

Interview a family member or other adult about a dramatic storm that he or she has experienced. Before the interview, make a list of questions you would like to ask. For example, how old was the person when the storm occurred? When and where did the storm occur? Write up your interview in a question-and-answer format, beginning with a short introduction.

Real-World Lab

Tracking a Hurricane

Hurricane alert! You work at the National Hurricane Center. It is your job to track the paths of hurricanes and try to predict when and where a hurricane is likely to strike land. Then you must decide whether to warn people in the area to evacuate.

Problem

How can you predict when and where a hurricane will come ashore?

Skills Focus

interpreting data, predicting

Materials

ruler
red, blue, green, and brown pencils
tracing paper

Procedure

1. Look at the plotted path of the hurricane on the map. Each dot represents the location of the eye of the hurricane at six-hour intervals. The last dot shows where the hurricane was located at noon on August 30.
2. Predict the path you think the hurricane will take. Place tracing paper over the map below. Using a red pencil, place an X on your tracing paper where you think the hurricane will first reach land. Next to your X, write the date and time you think the hurricane will come ashore.

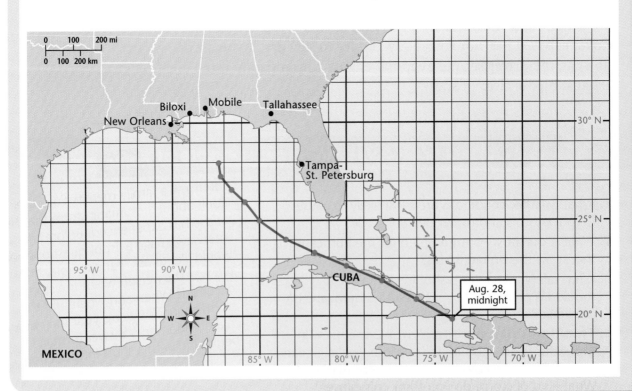

3. Hurricane warnings are issued for an area that is likely to experience a hurricane within 24 hours. On your tracing paper, shade in red the area for which you would issue a hurricane warning.

4. Using the following data table, plot the next five positions for the storm using a blue pencil. Use your ruler to connect the dots to show the hurricane's path.

Date and Time	Latitude	Longitude
August 30, 6:00 P.M.	28.3° N	86.8° W
August 31, midnight	28.4° N	86.0° W
August 31, 6:00 A.M.	28.6° N	85.3° W
August 31, noon	28.8° N	84.4° W
August 31, 6:00 P.M.	28.8° N	84.0° W

5. Based on the new data, decide if you need to change your prediction of where and when the hurricane will come ashore. Mark your new predictions in blue pencil on your tracing paper.

6. During September 1, you obtain four more positions. (Plot these points only after you have completed Step 5.) Based on these new data, mark in green pencil when and where you now think the hurricane will come ashore.

Date and Time	Latitude	Longitude
September 1, midnight	28.8° N	83.8° W
September 1, 6:00 A.M.	28.6° N	83.9° W
September 1, noon	28.6° N	84.2° W
September 1, 6:00 P.M.	28.9° N	84.8° W

7. The next day, September 2, you plot four more positions using a brown pencil. (Plot these points only after you have completed Step 6.)

Date and Time	Latitude	Longitude
September 2, midnight	29.4° N	85.9° W
September 2, 6:00 A.M.	29.7° N	87.3° W
September 2, noon	30.2° N	88.8° W
September 2, 6:00 P.M.	31.0° N	90.4° W

Analyze and Conclude

1. Describe in detail the complete path of the hurricane you tracked. Include where it came ashore and identify any cities that were in the vicinity.
2. How did your predictions in Steps 2, 5, and 6 compare to what actually happened?
3. What was unusual about your hurricane's path?
4. How do you think hurricanes with a path like this one affect the issuing of hurricane warnings?
5. Why do you have to be so careful when issuing warnings? What problems might be caused if you issued an unnecessary hurricane warning? What might happen if a hurricane warning were issued too late?
6. **Think About It** In this activity you only had data for the hurricane's position. If you were tracking a hurricane and issuing warnings, what other types of information would help you make decisions about the hurricane's path?

More to Explore

With your teacher's help, search the Internet for more hurricane tracking data. Map the data and try to predict where the hurricane will come ashore.

Hurricane Alert: To Stay or Not To Stay?

When a hurricane sweeps in from the ocean, the National Hurricane Center tracks the storm's course. Radio stations broadcast warnings. Sirens blow, and people in the storm path take steps to protect their homes and families.

State and local governments may try to keep people safe by closing state offices, setting up emergency shelters, and alerting the National Guard. As the danger increases, a state's governor can order the evacuation of people from dangerous areas. These actions are meant to protect public safety.

But not everyone wants to evacuate. Some people believe they have the right to stay. And officials cannot make people obey an evacuation order. How much can—or should—the government do to keep people safe?

The Issues

Why Play It Safe? Hurricanes can be extremely dangerous. High winds blow off roofs and shatter windows. Flash floods and storm surges can wash away houses. Even after the storm blows away, officials may need to keep people from returning home because of flooded sewers or broken power lines and gas mains.

In recent years, earlier and more accurate forecasts have saved lives. People now have time to prepare and to get out of the hurricane's path. Emergency officials urge people—especially the elderly, sick, or disabled—to leave early while the weather is still good. Most casualties happen when people are taken by surprise or ignore warnings. Those who decide to stay may later have to be rescued by boat or helicopter. These rescues add to the expense of the storm and may put the lives of rescuers in danger.

Why Ride Out the Storm? People have different reasons for not wanting to evacuate. Some want to protect their homes or businesses. Others don't want to leave pets or farm animals or go to public shelters. Store owners may stay open to sell disaster supplies. In addition, warnings may exaggerate the potential danger, urging people to leave when they might actually be safe. Since leaving can be expensive and disruptive, residents have to carefully evaluate the risks.

Is It a Matter of Rights? Should a government have the power to make people evacuate? Some citizens argue that the government should not tell them what to do as long as they are not harming others. They believe that individuals should have the right to decide for themselves. What do you think?

You Decide

1. Identify the Problem

In your own words, explain the controversy around hurricane evacuations.

2. Analyze the Options

Review and list the pros and cons of forcing people to evacuate. What people benefit? Who might be harmed? What more, if anything, should government officials do? What more could citizens do?

3. Find a Solution

Imagine that the radio has broadcast a hurricane warning. Write a dialogue in which you and members of your family discuss the options and decide whether or not to evacuate.

SECTION 3 Floods

DISCOVER

What Causes Floods?

1. Fill a cup with water. Hold a funnel above a basin and pour the water very slowly into the funnel.

2. Refill the cup with the same amount of water you used in Step 1. Hold the funnel above the basin and this time pour the water rapidly into the funnel. What happens?

Think It Over

Inferring How is a funnel like a river valley? What do you think would happen if a large amount of water entered a river valley in a short period of time?

A ntelope Canyon in the northern Arizona desert is only a few meters wide in places. On August 12, 1997, a group of 12 hikers entered the dry, narrow canyon. That afternoon a severe thunderstorm dropped several inches of rain on the Kaibeto Plateau, 24 kilometers away. Dry stream channels that drain into Antelope Canyon quickly filled with rainwater. The water rushed into the canyon, creating a wall of water over 3 meters high. Tourists at the top of the canyon watched in horror as the water swept the hikers away. Only one hiker survived.

Are you surprised that floods can occur in a desert? Actually, floods like this are more common in the dry Southwest than in areas with more rain.

GUIDE FOR READING

◆ What causes flooding?

◆ How can the dangers of floods be reduced?

Reading Tip As you read, draw a flowchart showing what can happen during a flood and how people should respond to it.

Figure 13 From the top, Antelope Canyon looks like a narrow slit in the ground.

① *Heavy rain falls on the plateau.*

② *Instead of soaking into the hard soil, the water runs into the canyon.*

③ *The rainwater is funneled into the narrow canyon and floods it.*

Figure 14 Flash floods occur when large amounts of rain are funneled into a narrow valley. This drawing shows what happened in the Antelope Canyon flood.

Flash Floods

Although movies feature the violent winds of tornadoes and hurricanes, floods are the most dangerous weather-related events in the United States. **Floods occur when so much water pours into a stream or river that it overflows its banks and covers the land on either side of the channel.** People who live along certain rivers know that melting snow and spring rains are likely to bring floods.

Unexpected floods are the most dangerous. Floods like the Antelope Canyon flood are called flash floods because the water rises very rapidly—"in a flash"—after it begins to rain heavily. A **flash flood** is a sudden, violent flood that occurs within a few hours, or even minutes, of a storm.

Most flash floods are due to large amounts of rain. For example, a line of thunderstorms may remain over an area, dropping heavy rain for several hours or days. Hurricanes or tropical storms bring downpours that quickly fill stream channels. A flash flood can also be caused by a dam breaking, releasing millions of liters of water all at once. Similarly, if ice that has jammed a river breaks free, the sudden rush of water can cause a flash flood.

✓ *Checkpoint* *Why are flash floods so dangerous?*

Flood Safety Measures

If you've never been in a flood, it's hard to imagine the awesome power of rushing water. What can people do to protect themselves and their homes?

Predicting Floods Advance warnings can help reduce flood damage and loss of life. Weather satellites supply information about snow cover so that scientists can estimate how much water will run into rivers when the snow melts. Radar can track and measure the size of an approaching rainstorm. Scientists check river gauges that measure water levels. With this information, forecasters can predict flood heights at different points along a river. Their goal is to issue warnings early enough to help people prepare and evacuate if necessary.

Sharpen your *Skills*

Communicating

Write a script for a 30-second public service radio announcement in which you tell about the dangers of floods. Include recommended safety steps to follow in case of a flood.

ACTIVITY

1

The car stalls in the water.

2

Moving water pushes against the car.

3

As the water rises, the car begins to float.

4

Sixty centimeters of water can wash a car away.

Figure 15 These drawings show what can happen to a car in a flood. *Applying Concepts Why is it dangerous to stay in a car in a flood?*

A "flood watch" is an announcement describing the area in which flooding is possible. Stay alert for more news. A "flood warning" is an announcement that floods have already been reported or are about to occur. It's time to take action!

Emergency Safety What should *you* do in case of a flood? When the danger becomes too great or the water rises too high, people are usually evacuated. **The first rule of flood safety: Move to higher ground and stay away from flood waters.** Don't try to cross streams and rivers that look as if they're flooded. Playing in flood waters may look like fun, but it's dangerous. A few centimeters of fast-moving water can sweep you off your feet. Even the storm drain on a city street can draw you in.

If your family is in a car, the driver shouldn't try to drive on a flooded road. Sometimes less than 60 centimeters of fast-moving water can sweep a car away, as shown in Figure 15. Everyone should leave the car and move to higher ground.

Figure 16 In the spring of 1997, the Red River of the North flooded regions of North Dakota and Minnesota. A large part of flooded downtown Grand Forks burned down because fire trucks could not get to the scene of the fire or connect to any fire hydrants.

Other Flood Hazards High water is not the only hazard in a flood. Floods can knock down electrical poles and wires, cutting off power supplies. Flood waters can also saturate soil, causing landslides or mudslides. If roads have been flooded or washed away, emergency vehicles such as fire trucks and ambulances may not be able to get through.

Flood waters can wash into wells and water treatment plants, polluting the water. Therefore, be careful with food and water that flood waters have touched. Boil water before drinking it to be sure it is safe.

Section 3 Review

1. How can precipitation cause flooding?
2. What should you do to stay safe during a flood?
3. What is the difference between a flood watch and a flood warning?
4. Name three tools that supply information used in forecasting floods and providing flood information.
5. **Thinking Critically** **Predicting** Describe two weather situations in which you would expect floods to occur.

Check Your Progress **CHAPTER PROJECT 3**
Now you are ready to predict tomorrow's weather. Look at today's weather map. Then predict tomorrow's weather both where you live and in the two other locations you selected. (*Project Hint:* Refer to the weather patterns you have been observing.) Decide what symbols you will need to use. Then, on an outline map of the United States, draw symbols to show what you think tomorrow's weather will be. Continue to make predictions every day for at least a week.

SECTION

4 Predicting the Weather

DISCOVER

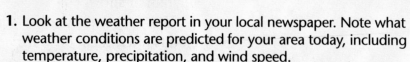

ACTIVITY

What's the Weather?

1. Look at the weather report in your local newspaper. Note what weather conditions are predicted for your area today, including temperature, precipitation, and wind speed.

2. Look out the window or think about what it was like the last time you were outside. Write down the actual weather conditions where you are.

Think It Over

Observing Does the weather report match what you observe? What is the same? What is different?

For centuries, people have tried to predict the weather. Every nation's folklore includes weather sayings. Many of these sayings are based on long-term observations. Sailors, pilots, farmers, and others who work outdoors are usually careful observers of clouds, winds, and other signs of coming changes in the weather. Here are two examples:

> *Evening red and morning gray*
> *Will send the traveler on his way;*
> *Evening gray and morning red*
> *Will bring down rain upon his head.*

> *Red sky in the morning,*
> *sailors take warning;*
> *Red sky at night, sailor's delight.*

Why do these two weather sayings agree that a red morning sky means bad weather? Recall that in the United States storms usually move from west to east. Clouds in the west may indicate an advancing low-pressure area, bringing stormy weather. If there are high clouds in the west in the morning, the rising sun in the east turns these clouds red. The reverse is true at sunset. As the sun sets in the west, it turns clouds in the east red. Clouds in the east may indicate that a storm is moving away to the east.

GUIDE FOR READING

◆ How does technology help forecasters predict the weather?

◆ What types of information are shown on weather maps?

Reading Tip Before you read, preview Figure 19 and *Exploring Newspaper Weather Maps.* Write a list of any questions you have about weather maps.

Chapter 3 **I ◆ 99**

Weather Forecasting

You can make many predictions from your own observations. For example, if a barometer shows that the air pressure is falling, you can expect a change in the weather. Falling air pressure usually indicates an approaching low-pressure area, possibly bringing rain or snow.

You can read weather signs in the clouds, too. Cumulus clouds often form on warm afternoons when warm air rises. If you see these clouds growing larger and taller, you can expect them to become cumulonimbus clouds, which may bring a thunderstorm. If you see thin cirrus clouds high in the sky, a low-pressure area may be approaching.

Even careful weather observers often turn to professional meteorologists for television weather information. You may hear the person who gives the television weather report referred to as a meteorologist. Despite their name, meteorologists don't study meteors. **Meteorologists** (mee tee uh RAWL uh jists) are scientists who study the causes of weather and try to predict it.

Meteorologists interpret information from a variety of sources, including local weather observers, instruments carried by balloons, satellites, and weather stations around the world. They use maps, charts, and computers to analyze the data and to prepare weather forecasts. Meteorologists use radar to track areas of rain or snow, so that forecasters can follow the path of a storm system.

Where do television and radio weather reporters get their information? A lot of weather information comes from the National Weather Service. However, weather forecasts for the general public may not have enough detail to be useful to farmers and pilots. There are also private weather-forecasting services, many of which use advanced, high-technology equipment. Private forecasting services are useful to people who need to answer questions like these: "Will the frost hurt the oranges in my orchard?" "Will the airport be fogged in?" "Will the trucks need to spread sand on the roads today?"

☑ *Checkpoint* *Where do meteorologists get weather information?*

Figure 17 These meteorologists are releasing a weather balloon. The box attached to the balloon contains instruments that will record weather data—such as temperature, pressure, and humidity—high in the troposphere.

Figure 18 This satellite photo shows an intense storm over the North Atlantic Ocean. *Observing* What weather-related information can you see in the photo?

Weather Technology

Techniques for predicting weather have changed rapidly in recent years. Short-range forecasts—forecasts for up to five days—are now fairly reliable. Meteorologists can also make long-range predictions that were once impossible. **Changes in technology have occurred in two areas: gathering weather data and using computers to make forecasts.**

Weather Balloons and Satellites As you learned in Chapter 1, weather balloons carry instruments high into the troposphere and stratosphere. The instruments measure temperature, air pressure, and humidity.

The first weather satellite was launched in 1960. Cameras on weather satellites in the exosphere can photograph Earth's surface, clouds, storms, and ice and snow cover. These images are then transmitted to meteorologists on Earth, who interpret the information.

Computer Forecasts Computers are widely used to help

INTEGRATING TECHNOLOGY forecast weather. Instruments can now gather thousands of bits of data about temperature, air pressure, wind speed, and other factors. Computers process large amounts of information quickly to help forecasters make predictions. To make a forecast, the computer starts with weather conditions reported from weather stations over a large area. Conditions reported include wind speed and direction, humidity, sunlight, temperature, and air pressure. Then the computer works through thousands of calculations and makes forecasts for 12 hours, 24 hours, 36 hours, and so on. Each forecast builds on the previous forecast. When new weather data come in, the computer revises its forecasts.

El Niño

Some long-term weather patterns may be caused by changes in ocean currents and global winds. Periodically, a warm-water event known as **El Niño** occurs in the tropical Pacific Ocean. During an El Niño event, winds shift and push warm surface water toward the west coast of South America. The warm water replaces the cold water that usually rises from the deep ocean near the coast.

El Niño events occur once every two to seven years. They can cause dramatic climate changes around the Pacific Ocean and in other places. In the winter of 1997 and 1998, a strong El Niño current caused droughts in Asia and Brazil, heavy rains and floods in California and Peru, and tornadoes in Florida and other parts of the southeastern United States.

Scientists have looked for clues and warnings to help predict the return of El Niño. One signal is rising surface temperatures in the tropical part of the Pacific Ocean. Using data gathered during past El Niño events, scientists were able to predict many of the results of the 1997–1998 El Niño.

☑ *Checkpoint* **What evidence do scientists use to predict an El Niño?**

Reading Weather Maps

A weather map is a "snapshot" of conditions at a particular time over a large area. There are many different types of weather maps. Television forecasters often present maps generated by computers from radar information.

Weather Service Maps Data from more than 300 local weather stations all over the country are assembled into weather maps at the National Weather Service. The information collected by a typical reporting station is summarized in the key to Figure 19. The weather map, which has been simplified, includes most of the weather station data shown in the key.

On some weather maps, you see curved lines. These lines connect places where certain conditions—temperature or air pressure—are the same. **Isobars** are lines joining places on the map that have the same air pressure. (*Iso* means "equal" and *bar* means "pressure.") The numbers on the isobars are the pressure readings. Air pressure readings may be given in inches of mercury or in millibars or both. Figure 19 has isobars.

Isotherms are lines joining places that have the same temperature. The isotherm may be labeled with the temperature in degrees Fahrenheit, degrees Celsius, or both.

Interpreting Data

ACTIVITY

Use the key to Figure 19 to help you answer the questions about this weather station data.

1. What is the temperature at this station?
2. What is the wind speed?
3. Which way is the wind blowing?
4. What is the air pressure?
5. What percent of the sky is covered by clouds?
6. What type of precipitation, if any, is falling?

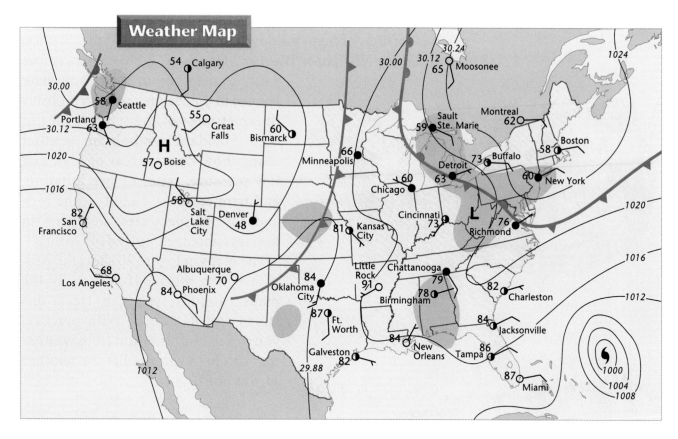

Weather Map

EXPLANATION OF FRONTS

▼▼▼ *Cold Front*
Boundary between a cold air mass and a warm air mass. Brings brief storms and cooler weather.

●●● *Warm Front*
Boundary between a warm air mass and a cold air mass. Usually accompanied by precipitation.

●●── *Stationary Front*
Boundary between a warm air mass and a cold air mass when no movement occurs. Brings long periods of precipitation.

▲▲▲ *Occluded Front*
Boundary on which a warm front has been overtaken by a cold front. Brings precipitation.

Weather	Symbol
Drizzle	❜
Fog	≡
Hail	△
Haze	∞
Rain	●
Shower	▽
Sleet	◬
Smoke	⌇
Snow	✳
Thunderstorm	⚡
Hurricane	◗

Wind Speed (mph)	Symbol
1–2	/
3–8	⌐
9–14	⌐
15–20	⌐
21–25	⌐
26–31	⌐
32–37	⌐
38–43	⌐
44–49	⌐
50–54	⌐
55–60	◢
61–66	◢
67–71	◢
72–77	◢

Cloud Cover (%)	Symbol
0	○
10	◐
20–30	◔
40	◑
50	◑
60	◕
70–80	◕
90	◑
100	●

How Symbols Are Used on a Weather Map

Amount of cloud cover (100%)

Atmospheric pressure (millibars)

Temperature (°F)

38 ● 1018

Wind direction (from the southwest)

Wind speed (21–25mph)

Figure 19 This weather map shows data collected from weather stations all over the country. Below the map is an explanation of what the symbols at each city mean.

Newspaper Weather Maps Maps in newspapers are simplified versions of maps produced by the National Weather Service. *Exploring Newspaper Weather Maps* shows a typical newspaper weather map. From what you have learned in this chapter, you can probably interpret most of the symbols on this map. **Standard symbols on weather maps show fronts, areas of high and low pressure, types of precipitation, and temperatures.** Note that the high and low temperatures are given in degrees Fahrenheit instead of Celsius.

The maps in Figure 20 show the path of a winter storm. If you study the maps carefully, you can track this storm and its effects. With practice, you can use information from weather maps to help you predict the weather in your area.

The Butterfly Effect

Even with current technology, weather forecasting is tricky. The main reason is that weather patterns do not follow an orderly, step-by-step process.

A forecast for the weather six days from now is based on forecasts for all the days between now and then. A small change in the weather today can mean a larger change in the weather a week later! This is the so-called "butterfly effect." The name refers to a scientist's suggestion that even the flapping of a butterfly's wings causes a tiny disturbance in the atmosphere. This tiny event might cause a larger disturbance that could—eventually—grow into a hurricane.

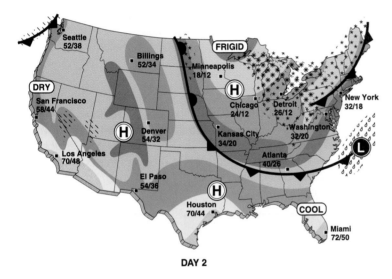

DAY 1

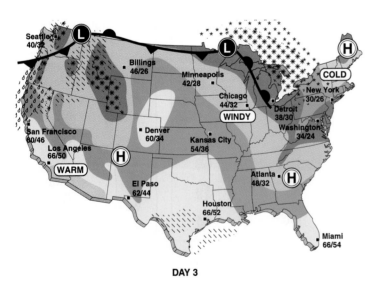

DAY 2

Figure 20 These weather maps show a storm moving from west to east over a three-day period.
Interpreting Diagrams What were the high and low temperatures in Chicago on Day 2? On Day 3?

DAY 3

EXPLORING Newspaper Weather Maps

Weather maps in newspapers use symbols to show fronts, high and low pressure areas, and precipitation. Color bands indicate different temperatures.

Major low-pressure areas are shown with an L. High-pressure areas are shown with an H.

Areas in the same temperature range are shown in the same color. For example, light green areas have high temperatures in the 40's.

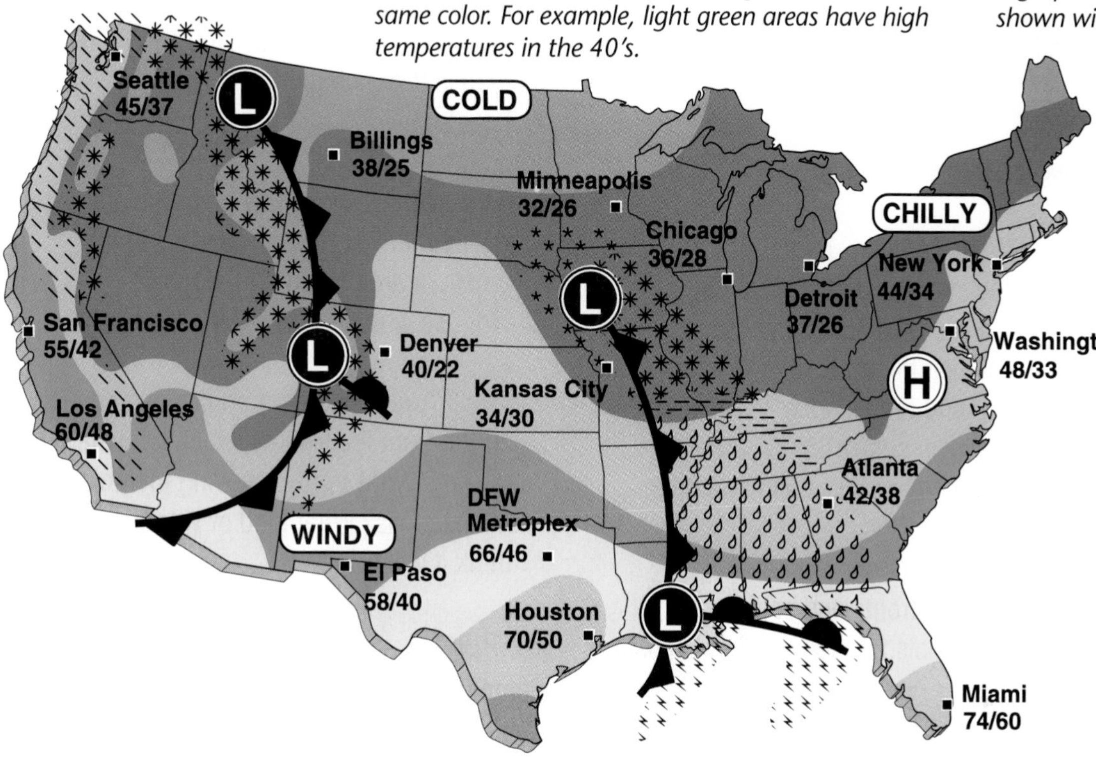

Seattle 45/37

COLD

Billings 38/25

Minneapolis 32/26

Chicago 36/28

CHILLY

Detroit 37/26

New York 44/34

San Francisco 55/42

Denver 40/22

Kansas City 34/30

Washington 48/33

H

Los Angeles 60/48

WINDY

DFW Metroplex 66/46

Atlanta 42/38

El Paso 58/40

Houston 70/50

Miami 74/60

Symbols that look like raindrops or snowflakes show precipitation.

The triangles showing a cold front point in the direction the cold air is moving. The half-circles indicating a warm front show the direction the warm air is moving.

Section 4 Review

1. What kinds of technology do meteorologists use to help predict the weather?
2. Name at least three types of information you could get from a weather map of your area.
3. What lines on a weather map connect points that have the same temperature?
4. **Thinking Critically** **Predicting** If you observe that air pressure is rising, what kind of weather do you think is coming?

Check Your Progress

CHAPTER PROJECT
3

After a week of predicting the weather, you are ready to compare your predictions to the actual weather that occurred. Then compare your predictions with those made by professional meteorologists. How accurate were your predictions? How accurate were the predictions made by professional meteorologists?

Reading a Weather Map

In this lab, you will interpret data from a weather map to describe weather conditions in various places.

Problem

How does a weather map communicate data?

Procedure

1. Examine the symbols on the weather map below. For more information about the symbols used on the map, refer to Figure 19 on page 103 and to *Exploring Newspaper Weather Maps* on page 105.
2. Observe the different colors on the weather map.
3. Find the symbols for snow and rain.
4. Locate the warm fronts and cold fronts.
5. Locate the symbols for high and low pressure.

Analyze and Conclude

1. What color represents the highest temperatures? What color represents the lowest temperatures?

2. What city has the highest temperature? What city has the lowest temperature?
3. Where on the map is it raining? Where on the map is it snowing?
4. How many different kinds of fronts are shown on the map?
5. How many areas of low pressure are shown on the map? How many areas of high pressure are shown on the map?
6. What season does this map represent? How do you know?
7. **Think About It** The triangles and semicircles on the front lines show which way the front is moving. What front is moving toward Minneapolis? What kind of weather do you think it will bring?

More to Explore

Compare this weather map with the weather map shown in a television news report. Which symbols on these maps are similar? Which symbols are different?

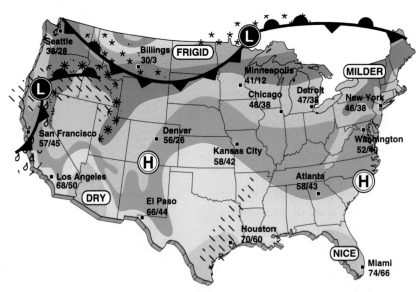

Air Masses and Fronts

Key Ideas

◆ Four major types of air masses influence the weather in North America: maritime tropical, continental tropical, maritime polar, and continental polar.

◆ When air masses collide, they form four types of fronts: cold fronts, warm fronts, stationary fronts, and occluded fronts.

◆ Cyclones and decreasing air pressure are associated with storms and precipitation.

Key Terms

air mass	maritime	occluded
tropical	continental	cyclone
polar	front	anticyclone

Storms

Key Ideas

◆ Thunderstorms and tornadoes form within large cumulonimbus clouds. During thunderstorms, avoid touching metal objects.

◆ A hurricane begins over warm water as a low-pressure area. If you hear a hurricane warning and are told to evacuate, leave the area immediately.

◆ Snow falls when humid air cools below 0°C. If you are caught in a snowstorm, try to find shelter from the wind.

Key Terms

storm	tornado	storm surge
lightning	hurricane	evacuate

Floods

INTEGRATING HEALTH

Key Ideas

◆ Floods occur when so much water pours into a stream or river that it overflows its banks on either side of the channel.

◆ The first rule of flood safety: Move to higher ground and stay away from flood waters.

Key Term
flash flood

 ## Predicting the Weather

Key Ideas

◆ Meteorologists interpret weather information from local weather observers, instruments carried by balloons, satellites, and weather stations around the world.

◆ Changes in weather technology have occurred in two areas: gathering weather data and using computers to make forecasts.

◆ Standard symbols on weather maps show fronts, areas of high and low pressure, types of precipitation, and temperatures.

Key Terms
meteorologist
El Niño
isobar
isotherm

Organizing Information

Compare/Contrast Table Copy the compare/contrast table about hurricanes and tornadoes onto a separate sheet of paper. Then fill in the empty spaces and add a title. (For more on compare/contrast tables, see the Skills Handbook.)

Type of Storm	Hurricane	Tornado
Where storm forms	Over warm ocean water	a. __?__
Size of storm	b. __?__	Several hundred meters
How long storm lasts	A week or more	c. __?__
Time of year	d. __?__	Spring, early summer
Safety rules	Evacuate or move inside a well-built building	e. __?__

Reviewing Content

 For more review of key concepts, see the Interactive Student Tutorial CD-ROM.

Multiple Choice

Choose the letter of the answer that best completes each statement.

1. An air mass that forms over an ocean is called
   a. tropical.
   b. continental.
   c. maritime.
   d. polar.
2. Cool, clear weather is usually brought by a
   a. warm front.
   b. cold front.
   c. stationary front.
   d. occluded front.
3. Winds spiraling inward toward a center of low pressure form a(n)
   a. anticyclone.
   b. front.
   c. isobar.
   d. cyclone.
4. Very large tropical storms with high winds are called
   a. hurricanes.   b. tornadoes.
   c. thunderstorms. d. blizzards.
5. Most flash floods are caused by
   a. hailstorms.   b. heavy rainfall.
   c. high winds.   d. melting snow.

True or False

If the statement is true, write true. If it is false, change the underlined word or words to make it true.

6. Summers in the Southwest are hot and dry because of <u>maritime tropical</u> air masses.
7. A <u>cold front</u> over an area will bring many days of cloudy weather.
8. Foggy, rainy, or humid weather usually follows the passage of a <u>warm front</u> through an area.
9. Low cumulonimbus clouds may bring both thunderstorms and <u>tornadoes</u>.
10. On a weather map, <u>isobars</u> join places on the map with the same temperature.

Checking Concepts

11. What are the basic characteristics used to describe air masses?
12. Describe how wind patterns affect the movement of air masses in North America.
13. How does a cold front form?
14. Describe three hazards associated with floods.
15. What are some of the sources of information that meteorologists use to predict the weather?
16. What is El Niño? How does it influence the weather in certain regions?
17. **Writing to Learn** Imagine you are a meteorologist. Your assignment is to investigate a hurricane by flying into it with a large plane. Describe your experiences in a journal entry. Be sure to include descriptive words. How did the hurricane look? Sound? Feel?

Thinking Critically

18. **Classifying** Classify the major types of air masses that influence weather in the United States in two ways: by temperature and by where they form.
19. **Comparing and Contrasting** Compare and contrast cyclones and anticyclones. What type of weather is associated with each?
20. **Applying Concepts** Would you expect hurricanes to form over the oceans off the northeast and northwest coasts of the United States? Explain.
21. **Relating Cause and Effect** How do differences in air density influence the movement of cold and warm fronts?
22. **Making Judgments** What do you think is the most important thing people should do to reduce the dangers of storms?

Applying Skills

Use the map to answer Questions 23–26.

23. Interpreting Maps Does the map show a cyclone or an anticyclone? How can you tell?

24. Interpreting Data What do the arrows show about the movement of the winds in this pressure center? What else indicates wind direction?

25. Making Models Using this diagram as an example, draw a similar diagram to illustrate a high pressure area. Remember to indicate wind direction in your diagram.

26. Posing Questions If you saw a pressure center like this on a weather map, what prediction could you make about the weather? What questions would you need to ask in order to make a better prediction?

Performance ▽ CHAPTER PROJECT 3 Assessment

Project Wrap Up Prepare your final report and arrange your maps for presentation. You may want to display each of your maps next to the actual newspaper weather map for that day. Practice your presentation, make any needed changes, and then present your report.

Reflect and Record In your journal, describe what you learned. Are there weather factors on the maps to which you should have paid more attention? Do meteorologists have information that isn't in the newspaper? How could you gather more information to improve your forecasting?

Test Preparation

Use these questions to prepare for standardized tests.

Read the passage. Then answer Questions 27–30.

As Hurricane Andrew roared toward the southern Florida coastline, millions of Florida residents evacuated the area, heading toward safety. It was 1992, and forecasters predicted that Andrew would make landfall sometime in the early morning of August 24. Andrew had been rapidly building speed and strength since it was first classified as a tropical storm on August 17. Andrew quickly advanced to a fierce Category 4 hurricane, with sustained wind speeds estimated at 145 m.p.h. The only type of hurricane that is stronger is a Category 5 hurricane—a very rare event.

Andrew pounded South Florida for several hours. In the end, this hurricane caused over $20 billion in damage to Florida, becoming the most expensive natural disaster in U.S. history up to that date.

27. What is the best title for this selection?
a. Category 4 Hurricanes
b. August 24, 1992
c. Hurricane Andrew Pounds Florida
d. Hurricane Andrew Heads North

28. What kind of storm was Andrew before it was classified as a hurricane?
a. tropical storm   b. thunderstorm
c. rainstorm   d. monsoon

29. Which category of hurricanes has the greatest wind speed?
a. category 1   b. category 4
c. category 5   d. none of the above

30. Why did Andrew cause so much damage?
a. because it traveled so fast
b. because it traveled in a northward direction
c. because it had very strong wind speed
d. because it traveled over water

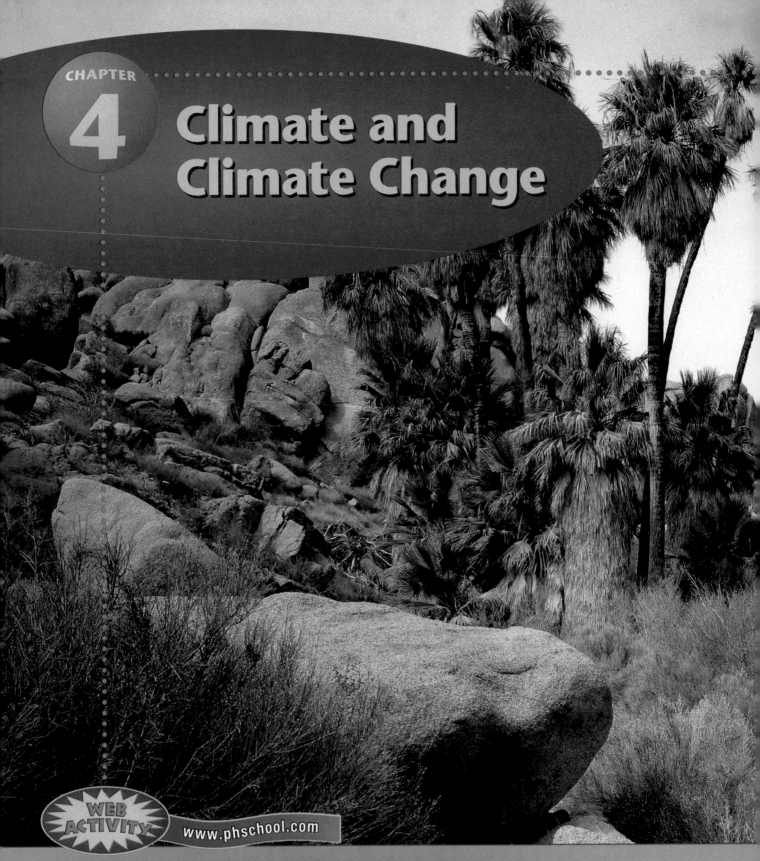

WEB
ACTIVITY
www.phschool.com

Investigating Microclimates

Most of the Mojave Desert is too dry for trees. Only cactus, shrubs, and other hardy plants are able to survive in the parched land. So if you see palm trees, you know there must be water nearby. Palm trees in the desert grow only in a small area with its own climate—a microclimate. As you work through this chapter, you will investigate microclimates in your community.

Your Goal To compare weather conditions from at least three microclimates.

To complete your project, you must
◆ hypothesize how the microclimates in three areas will differ from each other
◆ collect data at the same places and times each day
◆ relate each microclimate to the plants and animals found there
◆ follow the safety guidelines in Appendix A

Get Started Begin by brainstorming a list of nearby places that may have different microclimates. How are the places different? Keep in mind weather factors such as temperature, precipitation, humidity, wind direction, and wind speed. Consider areas that are grassy, sandy, sunny, or shaded. Start thinking about what instruments you will need to do your investigation.

Check Your Progress You'll be working on this project as you study this chapter. To keep your project on track, look for Check Your Progress boxes at the following points.
Section 1 Review, page 119: Measure and record weather data.
Section 3 Review, page 138: Graph your data and look for patterns.

Wrap Up At the end of the chapter (page 145), you will present the data you collected about your microclimates. Include any patterns you observed.

Even in a desert, palm trees can survive if they have enough water.

Integrating Environmental Science
SECTION 4 Global Changes in the Atmosphere

Discover What Is the Greenhouse Effect?
Try This It's Your Skin!

SECTION
1 What Causes Climate?

DISCOVER · ACTIVITY · · ·

How Does Earth's Shape Affect Climate Zones?

1. On a globe, tape a strip of cash register paper from the equator to the North Pole. Divide the tape into three equal parts. Label the section near the North Pole *poles*, the section near the equator *equator*, and the middle section *mid-latitudes*.

2. Tape the end of an empty toilet paper roll to the end of a flashlight. Hold the flashlight about 30 cm from the equator. Turn on the flashlight to represent the sun. On the paper strip, have a partner draw the shape of the area the light shines on.

3. Move the flashlight up slightly to aim at the section of the paper marked "mid-latitudes." Keep the flashlight horizontal and at the same distance from the globe. Again have a partner draw the shape of the area that the light shines on.

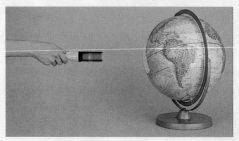

4. Move the flashlight up again to shine on the section of the paper marked "poles." Keep the flashlight horizontal and at the same distance from the globe. Draw the shape of the area that the light shines on.

Think It Over

Observing How does the shape of the area that is illuminated change? Do you think the sun's rays heat Earth's surface evenly?

GUIDE FOR READING

◆ What are the factors that influence temperature and precipitation?

◆ What causes the seasons?

Reading Tip As you read, use the headings to make an outline of the factors that affect climate.

I f you telephone a friend in another state and ask, "What's the weather there today?" she might answer: "It's gray, cool, and rainy. It's usually like that this time of year." Your friend has told you something about both weather and climate.

Weather is day-to-day events. The weather may be cloudy and rainy one day and clear and sunny the next. Weather refers to the condition of the atmosphere at a particular place and time. **Climate,** on the other hand, refers to the average, year-after-year conditions of temperature, precipitation, winds, and clouds in an area. How would you describe the climate where you live?

Two main factors—temperature and precipitation—determine the climate of a region. A climate region is a large area with similar climate conditions throughout. For example, the climate in the southeastern United States is humid, with moderate temperatures.

◀ These polar bears— two males and their mother—are taking it easy in the polar zone.

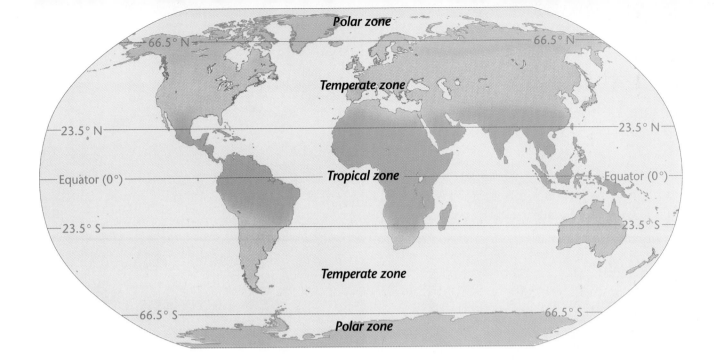

Figure 1 Earth has three main temperature zones.
Interpreting Maps In which temperature zone is most of the United States located?

Factors Affecting Temperature

Tropical countries, such as Panama, are usually hot. Northern countries, such as Finland, are usually cold. Why are some places warm and others cold? **The main factors that influence temperature are latitude, altitude, distance from large bodies of water, and ocean currents.**

Latitude In general, climates of locations farther from the equator are cooler than climates of areas closer to the equator. Why is this? As you found out if you tried the Discover activity, the sun's rays hit Earth's surface most directly at the equator. At the poles, the same amount of solar radiation is spread out over a larger area, and therefore brings less warmth.

Recall that latitude is the distance from the equator, measured in degrees. Based on latitude, Earth's surface can be divided into the three temperature zones shown in Figure 1. The **tropical zone** is the area near the equator, between about 23.5° north latitude and 23.5° south latitude. The tropical zone receives direct or nearly direct sunlight all year round, making climates there warm.

In contrast, the sun's rays always strike at a lower angle near the North and South poles. As a result, the areas near both poles have cold climates. These **polar zones** extend from about 66.5° to 90° north and 66.5° to 90° south latitudes.

The **temperate zones** are between the tropical and the polar zones—from about 23.5° to 66.5° north and 23.5° to 66.5° south latitudes. In summer, the sun's rays strike the temperate zones more directly. In winter, the sun's rays strike at a lower angle. As a result, the weather in the temperate zones ranges from warm or hot in summer to cool or cold in winter.

Figure 2 Mount Kilimanjaro in Tanzania, Africa, is near the equator. *Applying Concepts Why is there snow on top of the mountain?*

Altitude The peak of Mount Kilimanjaro towers high above the African plains. At nearly 6 kilometers above sea level, Kilimanjaro is covered in snow all year round. Yet it is located near the equator, at 3° south latitude. Why is Mount Kilimanjaro so cold?

In the case of high mountains, altitude is a more important climate factor than latitude. Recall from Chapter 1 that the temperature of the troposphere decreases about 6.5 Celsius degrees for every 1-kilometer increase in altitude. As a result, highland areas everywhere have cool climates, no matter what their latitude. At nearly 6 kilometers, the air at the top of Mount Kilimanjaro is about 39 Celsius degrees colder than the air at sea level at the same latitude.

Distance From Large Bodies of Water Oceans or large lakes can also affect temperatures. Oceans greatly moderate, or make less extreme, the temperatures of nearby land. Water heats up more slowly than land; it also cools down more slowly. Therefore, winds from the ocean keep coastal regions from reaching extremes of hot and cold. Much of the west coasts of North America, South America, and Europe have mild **marine climates,** with relatively warm winters and cool summers.

The centers of North America and Asia are too far inland to be warmed or cooled by the oceans. Most of Canada and Russia, as well as the central United States, have **continental climates.** Continental climates have more extreme temperatures than marine climates. Winters are cold, while summers are warm or hot.

Ocean Currents Many marine climates are influenced by ocean currents, streams of water within the oceans that move in regular patterns. In general, warm ocean currents carry warm water from the tropics toward the poles. Cold currents bring cold water from the polar zones toward the equator. The surface of the water warms or cools the air above it. The warmed or cooled air then moves over the nearby land. So a warm current brings warm air to the land it touches. A cold current brings cool air.

As you read about the following currents, trace their paths on the map in Figure 3. The best-known warm-water current is the Gulf Stream. The Gulf Stream begins in the Gulf of Mexico, then flows north along the east coast of the United States. When it crosses the North Atlantic, it becomes the North Atlantic Drift. This warm current gives Ireland and southern England a mild, wet climate despite their relatively high latitude.

In contrast, the cool California Current flows from Alaska southward down the West Coast. The California Current makes climates of places along the West Coast cooler than you would expect at their latitudes.

☑ *Checkpoint* **What effect do oceans have on the temperatures of nearby land areas?**

Sharpen your Skills

Inferring ACTIVITY

Look at the currents in the South Pacific, South Atlantic, and Indian oceans. What pattern can you observe? Now compare currents in the South Atlantic to those in the North Atlantic. What might be responsible for differences in the current patterns?

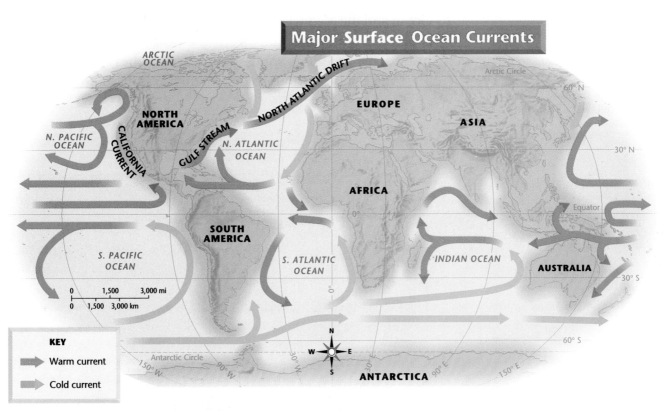

Figure 3 On this map, warm currents are shown in red and cold currents in blue.

Factors Affecting Precipitation

The amount of rain and snow that falls in an area each year determines how wet or dry its climate is. But what determines how much precipitation an area gets? **The main factors that affect precipitation are prevailing winds and the presence of mountains.**

Prevailing Winds As you know, weather patterns depend on the movement of huge air masses. Air masses are moved from place to place by prevailing winds, the directional winds that usually blow in a region. Air masses can be warm or cool, dry or humid. The amount of water vapor in the air mass influences how much rain or snow will fall.

Warm air can carry more water vapor than cold air can. When warm air rises and cools, water comes out of the air as precipitation. For example, surface air near the equator is generally hot and humid. As the air rises and cools, heavy rains fall, nourishing thick tropical forests. In contrast, sinking cold air is usually dry. Because the air becomes warmer as it sinks, it can hold more water vapor. The water vapor stays in the air and little or no rain falls. The result may be a desert.

The amount of water vapor in prevailing winds also depends on where the winds come from. Winds that blow inland from oceans carry more water vapor than winds that blow from over land. For example, the Sahara in Africa is near both the Atlantic Ocean and the Mediterranean Sea. Yet the Sahara is very dry. This is because few winds blow from the oceans toward this area. Instead, the prevailing winds are the dry northeast trade winds. The source of these winds is cool, sinking air from southwest Asia.

Figure 4 The prevailing winds that blow across the Sahara begin far inland. Since the air is dry, the Sahara gets very little rain.

SAHARA

AFRICA

ATLANTIC OCEAN

Mountain Ranges A mountain range in the path of prevailing winds can also influence where precipitation falls. As you have learned, when humid winds blow from the ocean toward coastal mountains, they are forced to rise up to pass over the mountains. The rising warm air cools and its water vapor condenses, forming clouds. Rain or snow falls on the **windward** side of the mountains, the side the oncoming wind hits.

By the time the air reaches the other side of the mountains, it has lost much of its water vapor, so it is cool and dry. The land on the **leeward** side of the mountains—downwind—is in a rain shadow.

The Owens Valley in California, shown in Figure 5, is in the rain shadow of the Sierra Nevada, about 80 kilometers west of Death Valley. Humid winds blow eastward from the Pacific Ocean. In the photo, you can see that this humid air has left snow on top of the mountains. Then the air flowed down the leeward side of the mountains. As it moved downward, the air became warmer. The desert in the Owens Valley, on the eastern side of the Sierra Nevada, was formed by this hot, dry air.

☑ *Checkpoint* *Why does precipitation fall mainly on the windward sides of mountains?*

Figure 5 The Sierra Nevada runs through eastern California, parallel to the Pacific coast. To the east of the Sierras is the Owens Valley, shown above. *Inferring Is the Owens Valley on the windward or leeward side of the mountains?*

Microclimates

Have you ever noticed that it is cooler and more humid in a grove of trees than in an open field? The same factors that affect large climate regions also affect smaller areas. A small area with specific climate conditions may have its own **microclimate.** Inland mountains, lakes, forests, and other natural features can influence climate nearby, resulting in a microclimate.

You might find a microclimate in a downtown area with clusters of tall buildings, or on a windy peninsula jutting out into the ocean. Even a small park, if it is usually sunnier or windier than nearby areas, may have its own microclimate. The grass on a lawn can be covered in dew and produce conditions like a rain forest, while the pavement in the parking lot is dry, like a desert.

Angles

Light from the sun strikes Earth's surface at different angles. An angle is made up of two lines that meet at a point. Angles are measured in degrees. A full circle has 360 degrees.

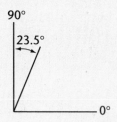

When the sun is directly overhead near the equator, it is at an angle of 90° to Earth's surface. A 90° angle is called a right angle. It is one fourth of a circle.

When the sun is near the horizon, it is at an angle of close to 0° to Earth's surface.

Earth's axis is tilted at an angle of 23.5°. About what fraction of a right angle is this?

The Seasons

INTEGRATING SPACE SCIENCE

Although you can describe the average weather conditions of a climate region, these conditions are not constant all year long. Instead, most places on Earth outside the tropics have four seasons: winter, spring, summer, and autumn.

You might think that Earth is closer to the sun during the summer and farther away during winter. If this were true, every place on Earth would have summer at the same time. Actually, when it is summer in the Northern Hemisphere it is winter in the Southern Hemisphere. So the seasons are *not* a result of changes in the distance between Earth and the sun.

Tilted Axis   *Exploring the Seasons* on page 119 shows how Earth's axis is tilted in relation to the sun. **The seasons are caused by the tilt of Earth's axis as Earth travels around the sun.** The axis is an imaginary line through Earth's center that passes through both poles. Earth turns, or rotates, around this axis once each day. Earth's axis is not straight up and down, but is tilted at an angle of 23.5°. The axis always points in the same direction— toward the North Star. As Earth travels around the sun, the north end of the axis is pointed away from the sun for part of the year and toward the sun for part of the year.

Winter or Summer   Look at *Exploring the Seasons* on the next page. Which way is the north end of Earth's axis tilted in June? Notice that the Northern Hemisphere receives more direct rays from the sun. Also, in June the days in the Northern Hemisphere are longer than the nights. The combination of more direct rays and longer days makes Earth's surface warmer in the Northern Hemisphere than at any other time of the year. It is summer.

In June, when the north end of Earth's axis is tilted toward the sun, the south end of the axis is tilted away from the sun. The Southern Hemisphere receives fewer direct rays from the sun. The days are shorter than the nights. As a result, the Southern Hemisphere is experiencing winter.

Now look at the situation in December, six months later. Which way is the north end of Earth's axis tilted now? The Northern Hemisphere receives fewer direct rays from the sun and has shorter days. It is winter in the Northern Hemisphere and summer in the Southern Hemisphere.

Twice during the year, in March and September, neither end of Earth's axis is tilted toward the sun. At both of these times, one hemisphere has spring while the other has autumn.

EXPLORING *the Seasons*

The seasons are a result of Earth's tilted axis. The seasons change as the amount of energy each hemisphere receives from the sun changes.

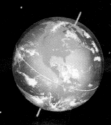
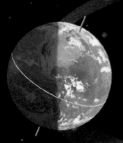
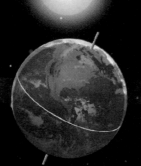

December
The south end of Earth's axis is tilted toward the sun. The Southern Hemisphere receives more energy from the sun. It is summer in the Southern Hemisphere and winter in the Northern Hemisphere.

June
As the north end of Earth's axis is tilted toward the sun, the Northern Hemisphere receives more energy. It is summer in the Northern Hemisphere and winter in the Southern Hemisphere.

March and September
Neither end of Earth's axis is tilted toward the sun. Both hemispheres receive the same amounts of energy.

Section 1 Review

1. Name the four main factors that influence the temperature of an area.
2. How do prevailing winds affect the amount of precipitation an area receives?
3. On which side of mountains—leeward or windward—does precipitation fall?
4. How does the tilt of Earth's axis cause the seasons?
5. **Thinking Critically Developing Hypotheses** How might Earth's climates be different if Earth were not tilted on its axis?

Check Your Progress

CHAPTER PROJECT 4

Have you chosen your micro-climate study sites? If your sites are on private property, get permission. Set up a logbook so that you can record your data. How do you think the conditions in these sites will differ? Write down your hypotheses. Now you are ready to measure daily weather conditions for your microclimates. (*Hint:* Be sure to take your measurements at the same time each day.)

Sunny Rays and Angles

In this lab, you will investigate how the angle of the sun's rays affects the amount of energy absorbed by different parts of Earth's surface.

Problem

How does the angle of a light source affect the rate of temperature change of a surface?

Materials

books   graph paper   pencil
watch or clock   ruler   clear tape
3 thermometers or temperature probes protractor
100-W incandescent lamp   scissors
black construction paper

Procedure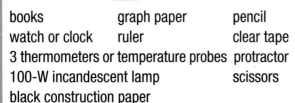

1. Cut a strip of black construction paper 5 cm by 10 cm. Fold the paper in half and tape two sides to form a pocket.
2. Repeat Step 1 to make two more pockets.
3. Place the bulb of a thermometer inside each pocket. If you're using a temperature probe, see your teacher for instructions.
4. Place the pockets with thermometers close together, as shown in the photo. Place one thermometer in a vertical position (90° angle), one at a 45° angle, and the third one in a horizontal position (0° angle). Use a protractor to measure the angles. Support the thermometers with books.
5. Position the lamp so that it is 30 cm from each of the thermometer bulbs. Make sure the lamp will not move during the activity.

6. Copy a data table like the one below into your notebook.
7. In your data table, record the temperature on all three thermometers. (All three temperatures should be the same.)
8. Switch on the lamp. In your data table, record the temperature on each thermometer every minute for 15 minutes. **CAUTION:** *Be careful not to touch the hot lampshade.*
9. After 15 minutes, switch off the lamp.

Analyze and Conclude

1. In this experiment, what was the manipulated variable? What was the responding variable? How do you know which is which?
2. Graph your data. Label the horizontal axis and vertical axis of your graph as shown on the sample graph. Use solid, dashed, and dotted lines to show the results from each thermometer, as shown in the key.
3. Based on your data, at which angle did the temperature increase the most?
4. At which angle did the temperature increase the least?

DATA TABLE

Time (min.)	Temperature (°C)		
	0° Angle	45° Angle	90° Angle
Start			
1			
2			
3			
4			
5			

5. What part of Earth's surface does each thermometer represent?
6. Why is air at the North Pole still very cold in the summer even though the Northern Hemisphere is tilted toward the sun?
7. **Think About It** In this experiment, what variables were held constant?

Design an Experiment

Design an experiment to find out how the results of this investigation would change if the lamp were placed farther from the thermometers. Then design another experiment to find out what would happen if the lamp were placed closer to the thermometers.

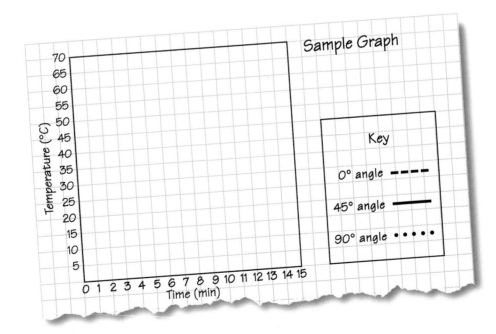

Sample Graph

Temperature (°C)

70
65
60
55
50
45
40
35
30
25
20
15
10
5

0 1 2 3 4 5 6 7 8 9 10 11 12 13 14 15
Time (min)

Key

0° angle   – – – –

45° angle ———

90° angle • • • • •

What Are Different Climate Types?

1. Collect pictures from magazines and newspapers of a variety of land areas around the world.

2. Sort the pictures into categories according to common weather characteristics.

Think It Over

Forming Operational Definitions Choose several words that describe the typical weather for each of your categories. What words would you use to describe the typical weather where you live?

GUIDE FOR READING

◆ What factors are used to define climates?

◆ What are the five main climate regions?

Reading Tip Before you read, preview *Exploring Climate Regions*. Write a list of any questions you have about climate regions.

When the Spanish settlers came to California in the 1700s, they brought with them plants from home. The padres, or priests, who established missions planted vineyards and orchards. They found that grapes, figs, and olives grew as well in California as they had in Spain. What do Spain and California have in common? They have similar climates.

Classifying Climates

The Spanish padres traveled a long distance but found a familiar climate. Suppose you traveled from your home to a place where the weather, the sunlight, and even the plants and trees were very different from what you are used to. Would you know what caused those differences?

Scientists classify climates according to two major factors: temperature and precipitation. They use a system developed around 1900 by Wladimir Köppen (KEP un). This system identifies broad climate regions, each of which has smaller subdivisions.

There are five main climate regions: tropical rainy, dry, temperate marine, temperate continental, and polar. Note that there is only one category of dry climates, whether hot or cold. These climate regions are shown in *Exploring Climate Regions* on pages 124–125.

◀ Olive trees

Exploring Climate Regions also shows a sixth type of climate: highlands. Recall that temperatures are cooler at the tops of mountains than in the surrounding areas. So a highland climate can occur within any of the other zones.

Maps show boundaries between the climate regions. In the real world, of course, no clear boundaries mark where one climate region ends and another begins. Each region blends gradually into the next.

☑ *Checkpoint* *What are the five main climate regions?*

Tropical Rainy Climates

The tropics have two types of rainy climates: tropical wet and tropical wet-and-dry. Trace the equator on *Exploring Climate Regions* with your finger. Tropical wet climates are found in low-lying lands near the equator. If you look north and south of tropical wet climates on the map, you can see two bands of tropical wet-and-dry climates.

Tropical Wet In areas that have a tropical wet climate, many days are rainy, often with afternoon thunderstorms. With year-round heat and heavy rainfall, vegetation grows lush and green. Dense rain forests grow in these rainy climates. **Rain forests** are forests in which plenty of rain falls all year-round. Tall trees such as teak and mahogany form the top layer, or canopy, while smaller bushes and vines grow near the ground. There are also many animals in the rain forest, including colorful parrots and toucans, bats, insects, frogs, and snakes.

In the United States, only the windward sides of the Hawaiian islands have a tropical wet climate. Rainfall is very heavy—over 10 meters per year on the windward side of the Hawaiian island of Kauai. The rain forests in Hawaii have a large variety of plants, including ferns, orchids, and many types of vines and trees.

Figure 6 Lush tropical rain forests grow in the tropical wet climate. *Relating Cause and Effect What climate factors encourage this growth?*

EXPLORING Climate Regions

Climate regions are classified according to a combination of temperature and precipitation. Climates in highland regions change rapidly as altitude changes.

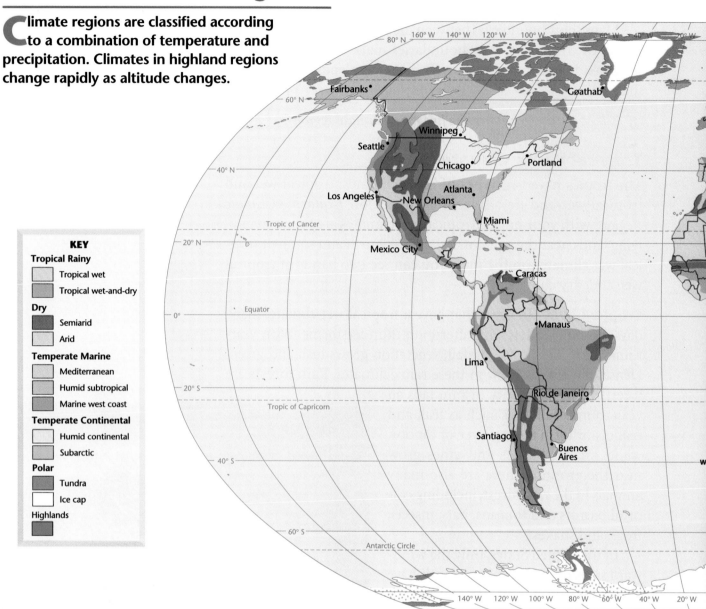

KEY

Tropical Rainy
- Tropical wet
- Tropical wet-and-dry

Dry
- Semiarid
- Arid

Temperate Marine
- Mediterranean
- Humid subtropical
- Marine west coast

Temperate Continental
- Humid continental
- Subarctic

Polar
- Tundra
- Ice cap

Highlands

Tropical Rainy
Temperature always 18°C or above.

Tropical wet *Always hot and humid, with heavy rainfall (at least 6 centimeters a month) all year round.*
Tropical wet-and-dry *Always hot, with alternating wet and dry seasons; heavy rainfall in the wet season.*

Dry
Occurs wherever potential evaporation is greater than precipitation. May be hot or cold.

Arid *Desert, with little precipitation, usually less than 25 centimeters a year.*
Semiarid *Dry but receives about 25 to 50 centimeters of precipitation a year.*

Temperate Marine
Average temperature 10°C or above in the warmest month, between –3° and 18°C in the coldest month.

Mediterranean *Warm, dry summers and rainy winters.*
Humid subtropical *Hot summers and cool winters.*
Marine west coast *Mild winters and cool summers, with moderate precipitation year round.*

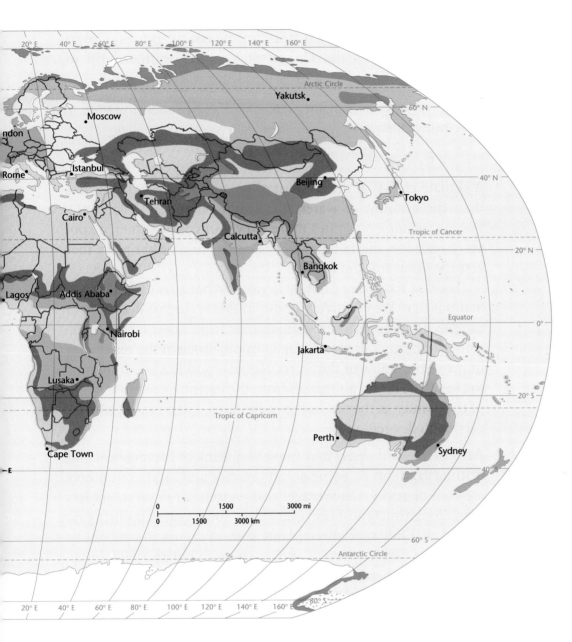

Temperate Continental
Average temperature 10°C or above in the warmest month, −3°C or below in the coldest month.

Humid continental *Hot, humid summers and cold winters, with moderate precipitation year round.*
Subarctic *Short, cool summers and long, cold winters. Light precipitation, mainly in summer.*

Polar
Average temperature below 10°C in the warmest month.

Tundra *Always cold with a short, cool summer—warmest temperature about 10°C.*
Ice cap *Always cold, average temperature at or below 0°C.*

Highlands
Generally cooler and wetter than nearby lowlands, temperature decreasing with altitude.

Figure 7 A reticulated giraffe gazes across the grasses and shrubby trees of the African savanna. Savannas are found in tropical wet-and-dry climates.

Tropical Wet-and-Dry Tropical wet-and-dry climates get slightly less rain than tropical climates and have distinct dry and rainy seasons. Instead of rain forests, there are tropical grasslands called **savannas**. Scattered clumps of trees that can survive the dry season dot the coarse grasses. Only a small part of the United States—the southern tip of Florida—has a tropical wet-and-dry climate.

☑ *Checkpoint* **What parts of the United States have tropical rainy climates?**

Dry Climates

A climate is "dry" if the amount of precipitation that falls is less than the amount of water that could potentially evaporate. Because water evaporates more slowly in cool weather, a cool place with low rainfall may not be as dry as a hotter place that gets the same amount of rain.

Look at *Exploring Climate Regions*. What part of the United States is dry? Why is precipitation in this region so low? As you can see, dry regions often lie inland, far from oceans that are the source of humid air masses. In addition, much of the region lies in the rain shadow of the Sierra Nevadas and Rocky Mountains to the west. Humid air masses from the Pacific Ocean lose much of their water as they cross the mountains. Little rain or snow is carried to dry regions.

Arid The word *desert* may make you think of blazing heat and drifting sand dunes. Some deserts are hot and sandy, but others are cold or rocky. On average, arid regions, or **deserts,** get less than 25 centimeters of rain every year. Some years may bring no rain at all. Only specialized plants such as cactus and yucca can survive the desert's dryness and extremes of hot and cold. In the United States there are arid climates in portions of California, the Great Basin, and the southwest.

Figure 8 Dry-land wheat farming is common in the steppe region of the Great Plains. *Comparing and Contrasting How are steppes similar to savannas, shown in Figure 7? How are they different?*

Semiarid Locate the semiarid regions on *Exploring Climate Regions*. As you can see, large semiarid areas are usually located on the edges of deserts. A steppe is dry but gets enough rainfall for short grasses and low bushes to grow. For this reason, a **steppe** may also be called a prairie or grassland.

The Great Plains are the steppe region of the United States. Many kinds of short grasses and wildflowers grow here, along with scattered forests. Livestock grazing is an important part of the economy of the Great Plains. Beef cattle, sheep, and goats graze on the short grasses of the region. Farm crops include grains, such as wheat and oats, and sunflowers.

Temperate Marine Climates

Look at *Exploring Climate Regions*, along the coasts of continents in the temperate zones. You will find the third main climate region, temperate marine. There are three kinds of temperate marine climates. Because of the moderating influence of oceans, all three are humid and have mild winters.

Marine West Coast The coolest temperate marine climates are found on the west coasts of continents north of 40° north latitude and south of 40° south latitude. Humid ocean air brings cool, rainy summers and mild, rainy winters.

In North America, the marine west coast climate extends from northern California to southern Alaska. In the Pacific Northwest of the United States, humid air from the Pacific Ocean rises as it hits the western slopes of the Coastal Ranges. As the air cools, large amounts of rain or snow fall on the western slopes.

Because of the heavy precipitation, thick forests of tall trees grow in this region, including coniferous, or cone-bearing, trees such as Sitka spruce, Douglas fir, redwoods, and Western red cedar. One of the main industries of this region is harvesting and processing wood for lumber, paper, and furniture.

TRY THIS

Modeling a Humid Climate

ACTIVITY

Here's how you can create humidity.

1. Put the same amount of water in each of two small plastic bowls.

2. Place a sheet of transparent plastic wrap over each bowl. Secure each sheet with a rubber band.

3. Place one bowl on a warm, sunny windowsill or near a radiator. Put the other bowl in a cool location.

4. Wait a day and then look at the two bowls. What do you see on the plastic wrap over each bowl?

Inferring Would you expect to find more water vapor in the air in a warm climate or in a cool one? Why? Explain your results in terms of solar energy.

Figure 9 Seattle, Washington, is in the marine west coast climate region. Here the summers are cool and rainy, and winters are wet and mild.

Figure 10 A. Much of Italy has a Mediterranean climate, with warm, dry summers and cool, rainy winters. **B.** Rice is a major food crop in places with a humid subtropical climate, as in parts of China. *Comparing and Contrasting How are Mediterranean and humid subtropical climates similar? How do they differ?*

Mediterranean A coastal climate that is drier and warmer than west coast marine is known as Mediterranean. Find the Mediterranean climates in *Exploring Climate Regions*. In the United States, the southern coast of California has a Mediterranean climate. This climate is mild, with two seasons. In winter, marine air masses bring cool, rainy weather. Summers are somewhat warmer, with little rain.

Mediterranean climates have two main vegetation types. One is made up of dense shrubs and small trees, called chaparral (chap uh RAL). The other vegetation type includes grasses with a few oak trees.

Agriculture is an important part of the economy of California's Mediterranean climate region. Some crops, including olives and grapes, were originally introduced by Spanish settlers. With the help of irrigation, farmers grow many different crops, including rice, oranges, and many vegetables, fruits, and nuts.

Humid Subtropical The warmest temperate marine climates are on the edges of the tropics. **Humid subtropical** climates are wet and warm, but not as constantly hot as the tropics. Locate the humid subtropical climates in *Exploring Climate Regions*.

The southeastern United States has a humid subtropical climate. Summers are hot, with much more rainfall than in winter. Maritime tropical air masses move inland, bringing tropical weather conditions, including thunderstorms and occasional hurricanes, to southern cities such as Houston, New Orleans, and Atlanta. Winters are cool to mild, with more rain than snow. However, polar air masses moving in from the north can bring freezing temperatures and severe frosts.

Mixed forests of oak, ash, hickory, and pines grow in the humid subtropical region of the United States. Cotton was once the most important crop grown in this region. Other crops, including oranges, grapefruits, peaches, peanuts, sugar cane, and rice, are now more important to the economy.

✓ *Checkpoint* **What is the main difference between a humid subtropical climate and a tropical climate?**

Temperate Continental Climates

Temperate continental climates are found on continents in the Northern Hemisphere. Because they are not influenced very much by oceans, temperate continental climates have extremes of temperature. Why do continental climates occur only in the Northern Hemisphere? The parts of continents in the Southern Hemisphere south of 40° south latitude are not far enough from oceans for dry continental air masses to form.

Humid Continental Shifting tropical and polar air masses bring constantly changing weather to humid continental climates. In winter, continental polar air masses move south, bringing bitterly cold weather. In summer, tropical air masses move north, bringing heat and high humidity. Humid continental climates receive moderate amounts of rain in the summer. Smaller amounts of rain or snow fall in winter.

What parts of the United States have a humid continental climate? The eastern part of the region—the Northeast—has a range of forest types, from mixed forests in the south to coniferous forests in the north. Much of the western part of this region—the Midwest—was once tall grasslands, but is now farmland. Farmers in the Midwest grow wheat, corn, other grains, and soybeans. These crops are used as food for people and for hogs, poultry, and beef cattle.

Subarctic The **subarctic** climates lie north of the humid continental climates. The world's largest subarctic regions are in Russia, Canada, and Alaska. Summers in the subarctic are short and cool. Winters are long and bitterly cold.

In North America, coniferous trees such as spruce and fir make up a huge northern forest that stretches from Alaska to Canada's east coast. Many large mammals, including bears, wolves, and moose, live in the forest. Small mammals such as beavers, porcupines, and red squirrels, and birds such as grouse and owls also live in the forest. Wood products from the northern forest are an important part of the economy.

Sharpen your Skills

Classifying

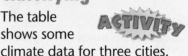

The table shows some climate data for three cities.

	City A	City B	City C
Average January Temperature (°C)	12.8	18.9	−5.6
Average July Temperature (°C)	21.1	27.2	20
Annual Precipitation (cm)	33	152	109

Describe the climate you would expect each city to have. Identify which city is Miami, which is Los Angeles, and which is Portland, Maine. Use *Exploring Climate Regions* on pages 124–125 to help identify each city's climate.

Figure 11 Subarctic climates have cool summers and cold winters. Parts of this region are called "spruce-moose belts."

Figure 12 Emperor penguins live on the ice cap of Antarctica.

Figure 13 The tundra is often very cold, but still many plants and animals live there. *Observing How are these musk oxen adapted to the cold climate?*

Polar Climates

The polar climate is the coldest climate region. Ice cap and tundra climates are found only in the far north and south, near the North and South poles.

Ice Cap As you can see in *Exploring Climate Regions*, ice cap climates are found mainly on Greenland and in Antarctica. With average temperatures always at or below freezing, the land in ice cap climate regions is covered with ice and snow. Intense cold makes the air dry. Lichens and a few low plants may grow on the rocks.

Tundra The **tundra** climate region stretches across northern Alaska, Canada, and Russia. Short, cool summers follow bitterly cold winters. Because of the cold, some layers of the tundra soil are always frozen. This permanently frozen tundra soil is called **permafrost.** Because of the permafrost, water cannot drain away, so the soil is wet and boggy in summer.

It is too cold on the tundra for trees to grow. Despite the harsh climate, during the short summers the tundra is filled with life. Mosquitoes and other insects hatch in the ponds and marshes above the frozen permafrost. Mosses, grasses, lichens, wildflowers, and shrubs grow quickly during the short summers. Herds of caribou and musk oxen eat the vegetation and are in turn preyed upon by wolves. Some birds, such as the white-tailed ptarmigan, live on the tundra year-round. Others, such as the arctic tern and many waterfowl, spend only the summer there.

✓ *Checkpoint* *What type of vegetation is found on the tundra?*

Highlands

Why are highlands a distinct climate region? Remember that temperature falls as altitude increases, so highland regions are colder than the regions that surround them. Increasing altitude produces climate changes similar to the climate changes you would expect with increasing latitude. In the tropics, highlands are like cold islands overlooking the warm lowlands.

The climate on the lower slopes of a mountain range is like that of the surrounding countryside. The foothills of the Rocky Mountains, for instance, share the semiarid climate of the Great Plains. But as you go higher up into the mountains, temperatures become lower. Climbing 1,000 meters up in elevation is like traveling 1,200 kilometers north. The climate higher in the mountains is like that of the subarctic: cool with coniferous trees. Animals typical of the subarctic zone—such as moose and porcupines—live in the mountain forest.

Above a certain elevation—the tree line—no trees can grow. The climate above the tree line is like that of the tundra. Only low plants, mosses, and lichens can grow there.

Figure 14 The top of this mountain is too cold and windy for trees to grow. *Classifying What climate zone does this mountaintop resemble?*

Section 2 Review

1. What two factors are used to classify climates?
2. Briefly describe each of the five main climate types.
3. Give three examples of how the climate of a region affects what plants and animals can live there.
4. **Thinking Critically Applying Concepts** Which of these two places has more severe winters—central Russia or the west coast of France? Why?
5. **Thinking Critically Classifying** Classify the main climate regions according to whether or not trees usually grow in each one.

Science at Home

Describe to your family the characteristics of each of the climate regions found in the United States. Which climate region does your family live in? What plants and animals live in your climate region? What characteristics do these plants and animals have that make them well-adapted to living in your climate region?

Careers in Science

Cool Climate Graphs

Real-World Lab

Y ou are a land-use planner who has been hired by a company that builds recreational facilities. Your company is considering buying land near at least one of four cities, all at about the same latitude. Your job is to decide which of the cities would be the best place to build a water park and which is the best place to build a ski-touring center.

Problem

Based on climate data, which city is the best place for each type of recreational facility?

Skills Focus

graphing, interpreting data, drawing conclusions

Materials

calculator
ruler
3 pieces of graph paper
black, blue, red, and green pencils
climate map on pages 124–125
U.S. map with city names and latitude lines

Procedure

1. Work in groups of three. Each person should graph the data for a different city, A, B, or C.
2. On graph paper, use a black pencil to label the axes as on the climate graph below. Title your climate graph City A, City B, or City C.
3. Use your green pencil to make a bar graph of the monthly average amount of precipitation. Place a star below the name of each month that has more than a trace of snow.
4. Use a red pencil to plot the average monthly maximum temperature. Make a dot for the temperature in the middle of each space for the month. When you have plotted data for all 12 months, connect the points into a smooth curved line.
5. Use a blue pencil to plot the average monthly minimum temperature for your city. Use the same procedure as in Step 4.
6. Calculate the total average annual precipitation for this city and include it in your observations. Do this by adding the average precipitation for each month.

Washington, D.C., Climate Averages

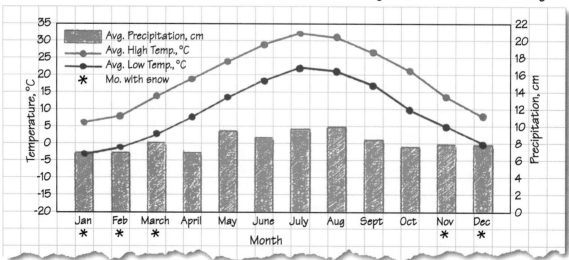

132 ◆ I

Climate Data

Washington, D.C.	Jan	Feb	Mar	April	May	June	July	Aug	Sept	Oct	Nov	Dec
Average High Temp. (°C)	6	8	14	19	24	29	32	31	27	21	14	8
Average Low Temp. (°C)	-3	-2	3	8	14	19	22	21	17	10	5	0
Average Precipitation (cm)	6.9	6.9	8.1	6.9	9.4	8.6	9.7	9.9	8.4	7.6	7.9	7.9
Months With Snow	*	*	*	trace	—	—	—	—	—	trace	*	*

City A	Jan	Feb	Mar	Apr	May	Jun	July	Aug	Sept	Oct	Nov	Dec
Average High Temp. (°C)	13	16	16	17	17	18	18	19	21	21	17	13
Average Low Temp. (°C)	8	9	9	10	11	12	12	13	13	13	11	8
Average Precipitation (cm)	10.4	7.6	7.9	3.3	0.8	0.5	0.3	0.3	0.8	3.3	8.1	7.9
Months With Snow	trace	trace	trace	—	—	—	—	—	—	—	—	trace

City B	Jan	Feb	Mar	Apr	May	Jun	July	Aug	Sept	Oct	Nov	Dec
Average High Temp. (°C)	5	7	10	16	21	26	29	27	23	18	11	6
Average Low Temp. (°C)	−9	−7	−4	1	6	11	14	13	8	2	−4	−8
Average Precipitation (cm)	0.8	1.0	2.3	3.0	5.6	5.8	7.4	7.6	3.3	2.0	1.3	1.3
Months With Snow	*	*	*	*	*	—	—	—	trace	*	*	*

City C	Jan	Feb	Mar	Apr	May	Jun	July	Aug	Sept	Oct	Nov	Dec
Average High Temp. (°C)	7	11	13	18	23	28	33	32	27	21	12	8
Average Low Temp. (°C)	−6	−4	−2	1	4	8	11	10	5	1	−3	−7
Average Precipitation (cm)	2.5	2.3	1.8	1.3	1.8	1	0.8	0.5	0.8	1	2	2.5
Months With Snow	*	*	*	*	*	trace	—	—	trace	trace	*	*

Analyze and Conclude

Compare your climate graphs and observations. Use all three climate graphs, plus the graph for Washington, D.C., to answer these questions.

1. Which of the four cities has the least change in average temperatures during the year?
2. In which climate region is each city located?
3. Which of the cities listed below matches each climate graph?

   Colorado Springs, Colorado   latitude 39° N
   San Francisco, California   latitude 38° N
   Reno, Nevada   latitude 40° N
   Washington, D.C.   latitude 39° N

4. Even though these cities are at approximately the same latitude, why are their climate graphs so different?
5. **Apply** Which city would be the best location for a water slide park? For a cross-country ski touring center? What other factors should you consider when deciding where to build each type of recreational facility? Explain.

More to Explore

What type of climate does the area where you live have? Find out what outdoor recreational facilities your community has. How is each one particularly suited to the climate of *your* area?

SECTION
3 Long-Term Changes in Climate

DISCOVER ·ACTIVITY· · · ·

What Story Can Tree Rings Tell?

1. Look at the photo of tree rings on page 135. Tree rings are the layers of new wood that form as a tree grows each year.

2. Look closely at the tree rings. Note whether they are all the same thickness.

3. What weather conditions might cause a tree to form thicker or thinner tree rings?

Think It Over
Inferring How could you use tree rings to tell you about weather in the past?

GUIDE FOR READING

◆ What principle do scientists follow in studying ancient climates?

◆ What changes occur on Earth's surface during an ice age?

◆ What theories have been proposed to explain natural climate change?

Reading Tip Before you read, preview the art and photos and read the captions. Write a prediction about how Earth's climate has changed through time.

One of the greatest Native American cultures in the American Southwest was the Ancestral Pueblos. These farming people built great pueblos, or "apartment houses," of stone and sun-baked clay, with hundreds of rooms. By about the year 1000, the Ancestral Pueblos were flourishing. They grew crops of corn, beans, and squash and traded extensively with other groups of people. But in the late 1200s, the climate became drier, reducing the size of their crops. After a long period of drought, the Ancestral Pueblos migrated to other areas.

Although weather can vary from day to day, climates usually change more slowly. But climates do change, both in small areas and throughout the world. Although climate change is usually slow, its consequences are great. Climate changes have affected many civilizations, including the Ancestral Pueblos.

Figure 15 The Ancestral Pueblos lived in these buildings, now in Mesa Verde National Park in southwestern Colorado, about 1,000 years ago.

Studying Climate Change

In studying ancient climates, scientists follow an important principle: If plants or animals today need certain conditions to live, then similar plants and animals in the past also required those conditions. For example, today magnolia and palm trees grow only in warm, moist climates. Scientists assume that the ancestors of these trees required similar conditions. Thus, 80-million-year-old fossils of these trees in Greenland are good evidence that the climate of Greenland was warm and moist 80 million years ago.

Tree rings can also be used to learn about ancient climates. Every summer, a tree grows a new layer of wood under its bark. These layers form rings when seen in a cross section, as shown in Figure 16. In cool climates, the amount the tree grows—the thickness of a ring—depends on the length of the warm growing season. In dry climates, the thickness of each ring depends on the amount of rainfall. By looking at cross sections of trees, scientists can count backward from the outer ring to see whether previous years were warm or cool, wet or dry. A thin ring indicates that the year was cool or dry. A thick ring indicates that the year was warm or wet.

A third source of information about ancient climates is pollen records. Each type of plant has a particular type of pollen. The bottoms of some lakes are covered with thick layers of mud and plant material, including pollen, that fell to the bottom of the lake over thousands of years. Scientists can drill down into these layers and bring up cores to examine. By looking at the pollen present in each layer, scientists can tell what types of plants lived in the area. The scientists can then infer that the climate that existed when the pollen was deposited was similar to the climate where the same plants grow today.

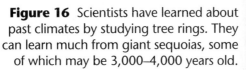

Figure 16 Scientists have learned about past climates by studying tree rings. They can learn much from giant sequoias, some of which may be 3,000–4,000 years old.

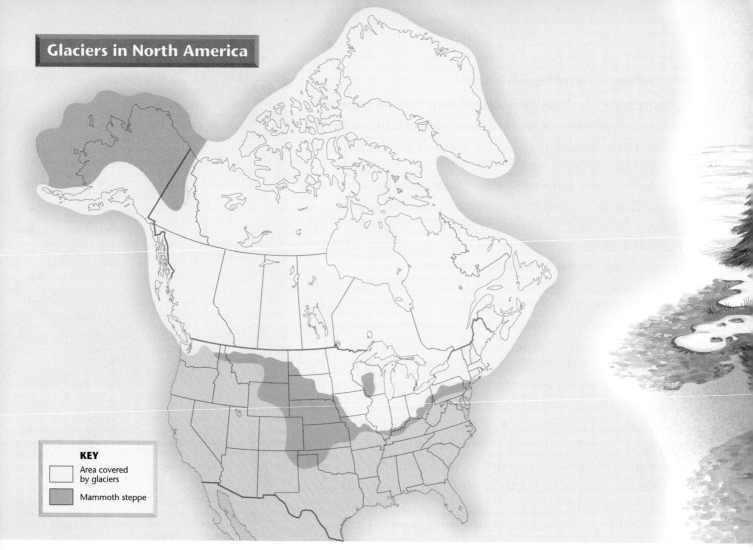

Figure 17 The map shows the parts of North America that were covered by glaciers 18,000 years ago. On the steppe near the glaciers lived many mammals that are now extinct, including woolly mammoths and scimitar-toothed cats.

KEY

☐ Area covered by glaciers

▨ Mammoth steppe

Ice Ages

Throughout Earth's history, climates have gradually changed. Over millions of years, warm periods have alternated with cold periods known as **ice ages,** or glacial episodes. **During each ice age, huge sheets of ice called glaciers covered large parts of Earth's surface.**

From fossils and other evidence, scientists have concluded that in the past two million years there have been at least four major ice ages. Each one lasted 100,000 years or longer. Long, warmer periods known as interglacials occurred between the ice ages. Some scientists think that we are now in a warm period between ice ages.

The most recent major ice age ended only about 10,500 years ago. Ice sheets covered much of northern Europe and North America, reaching as far south as present-day Iowa and Nebraska. In some places, the ice was more than 3 kilometers thick. So much water was frozen in the ice sheets that the average sea level was much lower than it is today. When the ice sheets melted, the rising oceans flooded coastal areas. Inland, large lakes formed.

☑ *Checkpoint* *Why were the oceans lower during the ice ages than they are now?*

Causes of Climate Change

Why do climates change? Scientists have formed several hypotheses. **Possible explanations for major climate changes include variations in the position of Earth relative to the sun, changes in the sun's energy output, and the movement of continents.**

Earth's Position Changes in Earth's position relative to the sun may have affected climates. According to one hypothesis, as Earth revolves around the sun, the time of year when Earth is closest to the sun shifts from January to July and back again over a period of about 26,000 years.

The angle at which Earth's axis tilts and the shape of Earth's orbit around the sun also change slightly over long periods of time. The combined effects of these changes in Earth's movements may be the main cause of ice ages.

INTEGRATING SPACE SCIENCE

Solar Energy Short-term changes in climate have been linked to changes in the number of **sunspots**—dark, cooler regions on the surface of the sun. Sunspots increase and decrease in regular 11-year cycles. Sunspot cycles could in turn be caused by changes in the sun's energy output.

Equator   Equator

Figure 18 The continents have moved over millions of years. *Interpreting Maps Which present-day continents broke away from Gondwanaland? Which broke away from Laurasia?*

Recently, satellite measurements have shown that the amount of energy the sun produces increases and decreases slightly from year to year. These changes may cause Earth's temperature to increase and decrease. More observations are needed to test this hypothesis.

Movement of Continents Earth's continents have not always been located where they are now. About 225 million years ago, most of the land on Earth was part of a single continent called Pangaea (pan JEE uh).

As Figure 18 shows, most continents were far from their present positions. Continents that are now in the polar zones were once near the equator. This movement explains how tropical plants such as magnolias and palm trees could once have grown in Greenland.

Over millions of years, the continents broke away and gradually moved to their present positions. The movements of continents over time changed the locations of land and sea. These changes affected the global patterns of winds and ocean currents, which in turn slowly changed climates. And as the continents continue to move, climates will continue to change.

Section 3 Review

1. What types of evidence do scientists use to study changes in climate?
2. How was the climate during an ice age different from the climate today?
3. List three factors that could be responsible for changing Earth's climates.
4. **Thinking Critically Predicting** What kinds of climate changes might be caused by a volcanic eruption? Would these changes be permanent? Explain.

Check Your Progress

CHAPTER PROJECT 4

What types of weather conditions have you measured at each site? Have you been recording all the data in your logbook? You should now be ready to graph and analyze your data. Are the weather conditions at all of your test areas similar, or do you see differences? What do you think causes the different conditions? What organisms did you observe at your sites?

SECTION 4 Global Changes in the Atmosphere

DISCOVER ● ACTIVITY ● ● ●

What Is the Greenhouse Effect?

1. Cut two pieces of black construction paper to fit the bottoms of two shoe boxes.

2. Place a thermometer in one end of each box. Read the temperatures on the thermometers. (They should be the same.) Cover one box with plastic wrap.

3. Place the boxes together where sunlight or a light bulb can shine on them equally. Make sure the thermometers are shaded by the sides of the boxes.

4. What do think will happen to the temperatures on the thermometers? Wait 15 minutes and read the thermometers again. Record the temperatures.

Think It Over

Inferring How can you explain the temperature difference between the box with the plastic wrap and the open box? Why does the inside of a car left in direct sunlight get so warm?

Have you ever seen a headline like the one below? If you hate cold winters and love summer sports, you may wonder what would be wrong with a slightly warmer world. Some experts agree with you, but many scientists are worried about such climate change.

> ✪ ANYWHERE U.S.A. DAILY NEWS ✪
> **Earth's Average Temperature Expected to Increase by 3 Celsius Degrees**

Most changes in world climates are caused by natural factors. In the last hundred years, however, human activities have also had an effect on Earth's climate and atmosphere. Two of the most important worldwide issues are global warming and thinning of the ozone layer.

Global Warming

Over the last 120 years, the average temperature of the troposphere has risen by about 0.5 Celsius degree. Was this increase part of natural variations, or was it caused by human activities? What effects could higher temperatures have? Scientists have done a great deal of research to try to answer these questions.

GUIDE FOR READING

◆ How might human activities be affecting the temperature of Earth's atmosphere?

◆ How have human activities affected the ozone layer?

Reading Tip As you read, draw a concept map showing how human activities can cause changes in the atmosphere and climate.

Sunlight

Infrared radiation cannot pass through greenhouse roof

Figure 19 Sunlight enters the greenhouse and is absorbed. The interior of the greenhouse radiates back energy in the form of infrared radiation, or heat. The heat is trapped and held inside the greenhouse, warming it. *Applying Concepts What gases in Earth's atmosphere can trap heat like a greenhouse?*

The Greenhouse Effect Recall that gases in Earth's atmosphere hold in heat from the sun, keeping the atmosphere at a comfortable temperature for living things. The process by which gases in Earth's atmosphere trap solar energy is called the greenhouse effect.

Gases in the atmosphere that trap solar energy are called **greenhouse gases.** Water vapor, carbon dioxide, and methane are some of the greenhouse gases. **Human activities that add greenhouse gases to the atmosphere may be warming Earth's atmosphere.** For example, the burning of wood, coal, oil, and natural gas adds carbon dioxide to the air. If the increased carbon dioxide traps more heat, the result could be **global warming,** a gradual increase in the temperature of Earth's atmosphere.

The amount of carbon dioxide in the atmosphere has been steadily increasing. Some scientists predict that if the level of carbon dioxide doubles by the year 2100, the average global temperature could go up by 1.5 to 3.5 Celsius degrees.

Another Hypothesis Not everyone agrees about the causes of global warming. Some scientists think that the 0.5 Celsius degree rise in global temperatures over the past 120 years may be part of natural variations in climate rather than a result of increases in carbon dioxide.

As you learned in Section 3, satellite measurements have shown that the amount of energy the sun produces increases and decreases from year to year. These changes in solar energy could be causing periods of warmer and cooler climates. Or climate change could be a result of changes in both carbon dioxide levels and amounts of solar energy.

Possible Effects Global warming has some potential advantages. Farmers in cool areas could plant two crops a year. Places that are too cold for farming today could become farmland. However, many effects of global warming are likely to be less positive. Higher temperatures would cause water to evaporate from exposed soil, such as plowed farmland. Dry soil blows away easily. Thus some fertile fields might become "dust bowls."

A rise in temperatures of even a few degrees could warm up water in the oceans. As ocean surface temperatures increased, the number of hurricanes might increase.

As the water warmed, it would expand, raising sea levels around the world. Glaciers and polar ice caps might partially melt, which would also increase sea levels. Sea levels have already risen by 10 to 20 centimeters over the last 100 years, and could rise another 25 to 80 centimeters by the year 2100. Even such a small rise in sea levels would flood low-lying coastal areas.

✓ *Checkpoint* *What are three possible effects of global warming?*

Ozone Depletion

Another global change in the atmosphere involves the ozone layer, which you learned about in Chapter 1. Ozone in the stratosphere filters out much of the harmful ultraviolet radiation from the sun.

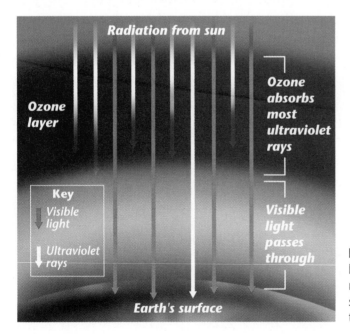

Figure 20 The ozone layer blocks much of the ultraviolet radiation coming from the sun. Visible light can pass through the ozone layer.

It's Your Skin!

ACTIVITY

How well do sunscreens block out ultraviolet rays? Here's how to compare sunscreens.

1. Close the blinds or curtains in the room. Place one square of sun-sensitive paper inside each of three plastic sandwich bags.

2. Place three drops of one sunscreen on the outside of one bag. Spread the sunscreen as evenly as possible. Label this bag with the SPF number of the sunscreen.

3. On another bag, repeat Step 2 using a sunscreen with a different SPF. Wash your hands after spreading the sunscreen. Leave the third bag untreated as a control.

4. Place the bags outside in direct sunlight. Bring them back inside after 3 minutes or after one of the squares of paper has turned completely white.

Drawing Conclusions Did both of the sunscreens block ultraviolet radiation? Did one of the sunscreens block more ultraviolet radiation than the other one? Explain your results.

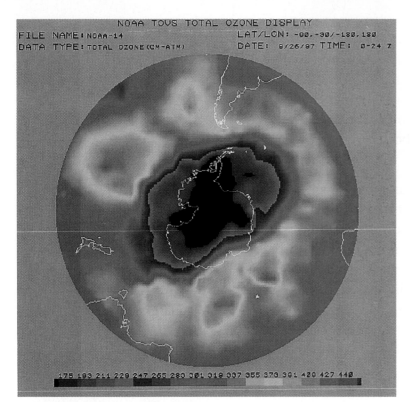

NOAA TOVS TOTAL OZONE DISPLAY
FILE NAME: NOAA-14   LAT/LON: -90,-30/-180,180
DATA TYPE: TOTAL OZONE(CM-ATM)   DATE: 9/26/97 TIME: 0-24 Z

175 193 211 229 247 265 280 301 318 337 355 373 391 409 427 440

Figure 21 This satellite image shows the concentration of ozone in the air over the South Pole. The dark area shows where the ozone layer is the thinnest.

In the 1970s, scientists noticed that the ozone layer over Antarctica was growing thinner each spring. By 1992, the area of thinner ozone was more than twice as large as the continental United States. What created the ozone hole? **Chemicals produced by humans have been damaging the ozone layer.**

The main cause of ozone depletion is a group of chlorine compounds called **chlorofluorocarbons,** or CFCs. CFCs were used in air conditioners and refrigerators, as cleaners for electronic parts, and in spray cans. Most chemical compounds released into the air eventually break down. CFCs, however, can last for decades and rise all the way to the stratosphere. In the stratosphere, ultraviolet radiation breaks down the CFC molecules into atoms, including chlorine. The chlorine atoms then break ozone down into oxygen atoms.

Because ozone blocks ultraviolet radiation, a decrease in ozone means an increase in the amount of ultraviolet radiation that reaches Earth's surface. If you have ever been sunburned, you can understand one effect of stronger ultraviolet radiation! Ultraviolet radiation can also cause eye damage and several kinds of skin cancer.

In the late 1970s, the United States and many other countries banned the use of CFCs in spray cans. In 1990, many nations agreed to end the production and use of CFCs by 2000. Because ozone depletion affects the whole world, such agreements must be international to be effective.

Section 4 Review

1. What human actions increase the amount of carbon dioxide in Earth's atmosphere?
2. How could increases in carbon dioxide in the air affect world temperatures?
3. What chemicals are the major cause of ozone depletion in the stratosphere?
4. **Thinking Critically Predicting** How might global warming change conditions where you live? How would this affect your life?

Science at Home

Visit a drugstore with your family. Compare the SPF (sun protection factor) of the various sunscreens for sale. Explain why it is important to protect your skin from ultraviolet radiation. Ask your family members to determine the best value for their money in terms of SPF rating and price.

CHAPTER 4 STUDY GUIDE

SECTION 1 What Causes Climate?

Key Ideas

◆ The climate of a region is determined by its temperature and precipitation.
◆ The main factors that influence temperature are latitude, altitude, distance from large bodies of water, and ocean currents.
◆ The main factors that affect precipitation are prevailing winds and the presence of mountains.
◆ The different seasons are a result of the tilt of Earth's axis as Earth travels around the sun.

Key Terms

climate	continental climate
tropical zone	windward
polar zone	leeward
temperate zone	microclimate
marine climate	

SECTION 2 Climate Regions

Key Ideas

◆ Climates are classified according to temperature and precipitation.
◆ There are five main climate regions: tropical rainy, dry, temperate marine, temperate continental, and polar. Highlands are often considered to be a sixth climate region.

Key Terms

rain forest	steppe	tundra
savanna	humid subtropical	permafrost
desert	subarctic	

SECTION 3 Long-Term Changes in Climate

Key Ideas

◆ During each ice age, huge sheets of ice covered much of Earth's surface.
◆ Possible explanations for major climate changes include movement of continents, variations in the position of Earth relative to the sun, and changes in the sun's energy output.

Key Terms

ice age   sunspot

SECTION 4 Global Changes in the Atmosphere

INTEGRATING ENVIRONMENTAL SCIENCE

Key Ideas

◆ Human activities that add greenhouse gases to the atmosphere may be warming Earth's atmosphere.
◆ Chemicals produced by humans have been damaging the ozone layer.

Key Terms

greenhouse gas
global warming
chlorofluorocarbons

Organizing Information

Concept Map Copy the concept map about climate onto a separate sheet of paper. Then complete it and add a title. (For more on concept maps, see the Skills Handbook.)

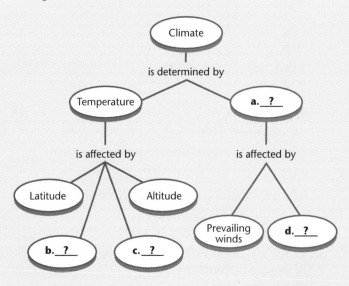

Reviewing Content

 For more review of key concepts, see the Interactive Student Tutorial CD-ROM.

Multiple Choice

Choose the letter of the best answer.

1. Temperatures are highest in the tropical zone because
   a. the land is flat.
   b. the sun's rays strike most directly.
   c. Earth's axis is tilted toward the sun.
   d. ocean currents warm the region.
2. Continental climates are found
   a. on every continent.
   b. only near the equator.
   c. only in the Northern Hemisphere.
   d. only in the Southern Hemisphere.
3. In a wet-and-dry tropical climate, the most common vegetation is
   a. coniferous forests.
   b. savanna grasslands.
   c. tropical rain forest.
   d. steppe grasslands.
4. Extremely cold periods in Earth's history have resulted in huge
   a. tree rings.
   b. sunspots.
   c. pollen deposits.
   d. glaciers.
5. Chlorofluorocarbons, or CFCs, are the main cause of
   a. ozone depletion.
   b. global warming.
   c. the greenhouse effect.
   d. ice ages.

True or False

If the statement is true, write true. If it is false, change the underlined word or words to make it true.

6. The prevailing winds affect how much <u>sunlight</u> falls on an area.
7. When the north end of Earth's axis is tilted toward the sun, it is <u>summer</u> in the Southern Hemisphere.
8. Climate regions are classified according to temperature and <u>precipitation</u>.
9. A <u>thin</u> tree ring indicates that a year was cool or dry.
10. An increase in <u>nitrogen</u> in the atmosphere may be making world temperatures increase.

Checking Concepts

11. Explain how distance from large bodies of water can affect the temperature of nearby land areas.
12. What causes Earth's seasons?
13. Identify the parts of the United States that are located in each of the three temperature zones.
14. How are "dry" climates defined? How do the two types of dry climate differ?
15. How does the movement of continents explain major changes in climate over time?
16. To be effective, why must agreements aimed at preventing or reducing ozone depletion be international?
17. **Writing to Learn** In what climate region do you live? Write a description of your local climate and identify some of the things—such as latitude, bodies of water, or wind patterns—that affect the climate.

Thinking Critically

18. **Relating Cause and Effect** Describe three ways in which water influences climate.
19. **Comparing and Contrasting** How is global warming different from earlier changes in Earth's climate?
20. **Making Judgments** What is the most important thing that needs to be done about global warming?
21. **Relating Cause and Effect** Why do parts of the United States have a semiarid climate while neighboring areas have a humid continental climate?

Applying Skills

Use the map of world temperature zones to answer Questions 22–24.

22. Interpreting Maps Name each of the five zones shown on the map.

23. Measuring What is the name of the temperature zone that includes the equator? How many degrees of latitude does this zone cover?

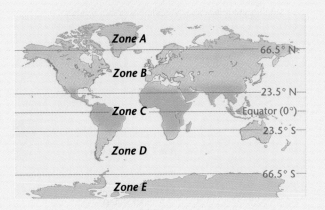

24. Interpreting Data Which of the five zones shown on the map has the greatest amount of land area suitable for people to live?

CHAPTER PROJECT 4
Performance **Assessment**

Project Wrap Up Decide how to present your project. You could use a written report, oral presentation, or a bulletin board. Do your graphs compare the conditions in the different microclimates? What conditions favor plants or animals in some areas? After you present your project to the class, discuss what you think causes different microclimates.

Reflect and Record In your journal, describe how you could improve your investigation. Are there factors you did not study? Did you notice any organisms that live only in certain microclimates? What additional information about microclimates would you like to find?

Test Preparation
Use these questions to prepare for standardized tests.

Study the graph. Then answer Questions 25–30.

25. Which of the following months has the widest range of temperatures during the year?
a. September   b. June
c. May   d. April

26. Which month shown on the graph is the warmest on average?
a. August   b. June
c. July   d. May

27. Which month is the coldest on average?
a. January   b. December
c. March   d. February

28. What is the average temperature in April?
a. about −21°C   b. about −17°C
c. about 0°C   d. about −30°C

29. What is the average temperature in December?
a. about −20°C   b. about −26°C
c. about 0°C   d. about −30°C

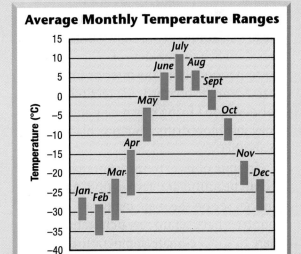

30. What kind of climate is indicated by the graph?
a. polar
b. temperate continental
c. temperate marine
d. tropical rainy

ANTARCTICA

What kind of weather do you expect in July—hot and sunny? Brace yourself—July in Antarctica will surprise you!

On July 21, 1983, the temperature at the Russian research station Vostok dropped to a world record low: –89°C.

WELCOME TO ANTARCTICA!

Because Antarctica is in the Southern Hemisphere, July is midwinter there. But the temperature isn't very warm in summer, either. The average summer temperature at Vostok is –33°C. Antarctica's climate is unusual in other ways. It's the windiest continent as well as the coldest. Even though Antarctica is covered with snow and ice, it's also the driest continent—a snowy desert. Less than five centimeters of precipitation falls in the interior in a year. Antarctic blizzards are terrifying, but they don't bring much new snow. They just blow drifts from one place to another.

In spite of its extremes, Antarctica is both beautiful and fascinating. As you can see on the map, many countries have set up research stations there to study climate, temperature, and the atmosphere. Scientists in Antarctica also research wildlife and geology.

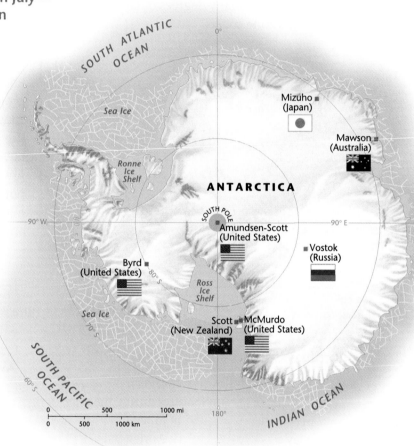

The map shows major research stations in Antarctica.

A huge dome covers buildings at the U.S. Amundsen-Scott station at the South Pole.

Race to the South Pole

Would you brave the darkness and cold of Antarctica? In the early 1900s, several famous explorers began a "race to the pole." Their attempts to reach the South Pole produced stories of heroism—and tragedy.

Robert F. Scott (above center) and his men reached the South Pole, but lost the race.

In October 1911, the British explorer Robert Falcon Scott traveled to the South Pole. He started overland with dog teams, motorized sleds, and ponies. He and four other explorers reached the South Pole in January 1912—only to find that a Norwegian expedition led by Roald Amundsen had beaten them there by a month! Scott's team had lost the race!

Soon after, Scott and his crew started back. But they were trapped in blizzards. All of them died. Searchers later found their tent, Scott's diary, and photographs. Scott's team had been only 18 kilometers from a supply camp.

A few years later, Sir Ernest Shackleton was the hero of an incredible Antarctic survival story. In 1914, Shackleton tried a new route to the South Pole. On the way, ice trapped and crushed his ship, the *Endurance*. He and his men escaped across the ice to Elephant Island. Leaving 22 men there, Shackleton and five others sailed in a small whaleboat to find help. Amazingly, everyone was rescued.

In the 1920s, airplanes brought a new way to explore Antarctica. American pilot and explorer Richard E. Byrd led the first flight over the South Pole in 1929. Later, Byrd set up research stations at Little America.

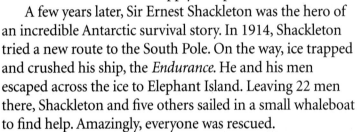

Social Studies Activity

Create a time line of important events in Antarctica. Find photos or draw sketches to illustrate the events.
Include the following events:
- early expeditions
- "race to the pole" in the early 1900s
- International Geophysical Year
- Antarctic Treaty
- new research stations

Why did it take courage and endurance to try to reach the South Pole in the early 1900s?

International Cooperation

In 1957–1958, during the International Geophysical Year, scientists from countries around the world established research stations in Antarctica and shared their scientific findings. In 1959, twelve nations signed the Antarctic Treaty to guarantee "freedom of scientific investigation." The original signers were (from top left) Argentina, Australia, Belgium, Chile, France, Japan, New Zealand, Norway, the Soviet Union, South Africa, the United Kingdom, and the United States.

Science

Continent of Extremes

Why is Antarctica so cold? Its high latitude and months of darkness are important reasons. In addition, the broad expanses of white snow and icy glaciers reflect back sunlight before much heat is absorbed.

As on every continent, climates vary from place to place. Warmer parts of Antarctica are at lower elevations, at lower latitudes, or near the coast. Coastal areas are warmer because the nearby ocean moderates temperatures. These areas also have bare land, which absorbs heat.

Summer weather patterns in Antarctica are different from winter patterns. The short summer warm-up starts in October. The warmest temperatures are from mid-December to mid-January. Then temperatures drop suddenly. So by mid-March, the beginning of winter, the temperature has fallen to winter levels. Over the next six months Antarctica remains very cold—and dark.

Science Activity

Staying warm is essential for life in the Antarctic. Set up an experiment to test how well different materials keep heat from escaping. Use socks made of nylon, silk, cotton, and wool. You will need a jar for each material plus one jar as a control.

- ◆ Fill jars with equal amounts of very hot water. The water in each jar should be the same temperature.
- ◆ Record the temperature of each jar and screw each cap on.
- ◆ Place each jar, except the control, inside a sock. Refrigerate all the jars for 30 minutes.
- ◆ Remove the jars and record the water temperature of each.

Which jar cooled fastest? Which materials retained the heat best?

How do polar explorers and researchers stay warm? The secret is wearing layers of clothing that keep body heat from escaping. ▼

An insulated hood, a hat with earflaps, or a face mask protects against wind. Sunglasses or goggles reduce the glare of sunlight and protect eyes from freezing.

Boots and gloves are layered, too. A layer of fleece may be sealed inside a waterproof rubber layer.

- • An **inner layer** of long underwear (silk, wool, or synthetic) carries moisture away from the skin.

- • A fluffy **insulating layer,** such as fleece or down, traps pockets of air that are warmed by body heat.

- • The **outer shell layer** protects against wind and water.

**Lingering
Antarctic sunset**

Sky Watch

It's March 21—the beginning of winter—
and you're watching the sun set very,
very slowly. It takes 30 hours—more
than a day—for the sun to disappear
below the horizon. Once it's gone, you
won't see sunshine again until
September! April and early May aren't
completely dark, but there is hardly
enough light to cast a shadow. Then it's
dark for two months. In August, light
begins again. The sky brightens quickly
until the polar sunrise.

The tilt of Earth on its axis affects
the hours of daylight and darkness
from season to season. At the poles,
midsummer brings the "midnight
sun," which circles around the sky but
does not set. Midwinter brings almost
total darkness.

The table shows hours of daylight on ▶
the 15th of each month. It shows
readings at two different Antarctic
locations—the Amundsen-Scott
station and Japan's Mizuho station.

HOURS OF DAYLIGHT IN ANTARCTICA
(sunrise to sunset, rounded to nearest hour)

Month	Mizuho Station 70° S	Amundsen-Scott Station 90° S
January	24	24
February	18	24
March	14	24
April	9	0
May	3	0
June	0	0
July	0	0
August	7	0
September	11	0
October	16	24
November	22	24
December	24	24

Math Activity

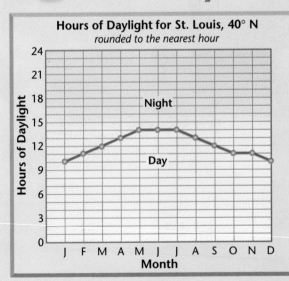

Hours of Daylight for St. Louis, 40° N
rounded to the nearest hour

(Graph: Hours of Daylight vertical axis 0 to 24; Month horizontal axis J F M A M J J A S O N D; labeled "Night" and "Day")

This line graph shows the year-round pattern of
daylight for St. Louis, Missouri, located at about
40° north latitude. Readings were taken on the
fifteenth of each month. Use the table to make
another line graph that shows hours of daylight for
Mizuho station, Amundsen-Scott station, and St. Louis.

◆ On the horizontal axis of the table, list the months.

◆ On the vertical axis, mark off spaces for 0 to
24 hours.

◆ Choose a different color marker for each latitude.
Above each month for each location, place a colored
dot at the correct hour mark. Connect the dots to
show changes in daylight at each place during a year.

◆ How are the changes in darkness and daylight in
Antarctica like those you see at home? How are they
different?

Alone in Antarctica

Admiral Richard Byrd worked in the Antarctic for nearly 30 years after his flight over the South Pole. He led several expeditions and set up research stations at Little America. Byrd's book *Alone* is based on the journal he kept while spending the winter of 1934 alone at a weather station outpost. During his four-and-a-half-month stay, Byrd nearly gave up mentally and physically. He endured, however, and kept up his weather research until help arrived in August.

   In this memoir of his days in early April, 1934, Byrd describes some of the problems of working in the intense cold.

At times I felt as if I were the last survivor of an Ice Age, striving to hold on with the flimsy tools bequeathed by an easy-going, temperate world. Cold does queer things. At 50° Fahrenheit below zero a flashlight dies out in your hand. At −55° Fahrenheit kerosene will freeze, and the flame will dry up on the wick. At −60° Fahrenheit rubber turns brittle. One day, I remember, the antenna wire snapped in my hands when I tried to bend it to make a new connection. Below −60° Fahrenheit cold will find the last microscopic touch of oil in an instrument and stop it dead. If there is the slightest breeze, you can hear your breath freeze as it floats away, making a sound like that of Chinese firecrackers. . . . And if you work too hard and breathe too deeply, your lungs will sometimes feel as if they were on fire.

   Cold—even April's relatively moderate cold— gave me plenty to think about. . . . Two cases of tomato juice shattered their bottles. Whenever I brought canned food inside the shack I had to let it stand all day near the stove to thaw. . . . Frost was forever collecting on the electrical contact points of

Admiral Byrd tries to keep warm in his small shack at Little America. ▶

Coastal view of Antarctica ▼

the wind vane and wind cups. Some days I climbed the twelve-foot anemometer pole two and three times to clean them. It was a bitter job, especially on blustery nights. With my legs twined around the slender pole, my arms flung over the cleats, and my free hands trying to scrape the contact point clean with a knife and at the same time hold a flashlight to see, I qualified for the world's coldest flagpole sitter. I seldom came down from that pole without a frozen finger, toe, nose, or cheek.

The shack was always freezingly cold in the morning. I slept with the door open [for ventilation]. When I arose the inside temperature (depending upon the surface weather) might be anywhere from 10° to 40° Fahrenheit below zero. Frost coated the sleeping bag where my breath had condensed during the night; my socks and boots, when I picked them up, were so stiff with frozen sweat that I first had to work them between my hands. A pair of silk gloves hung from a nail over the bunk, where I could grab them the first thing. Yet, even with their protection, my fingers would sting and burn from the touch of the lamp and stove as I lighted them.

Language Arts Activity

From this passage, what can you conclude about Byrd's attitude toward his research? Although you've probably never traveled to Antarctica, you may have had an outdoor adventure—at summer camp or even in a city park. Use descriptive writing to recapture that experience. Remember to include concrete, sensory details like those in Byrd's journal. If you prefer, write about an imaginary event or adventure in the outdoors.

Tie It Together

Plan a Cool Expedition

You're on your way to Antarctica! Good planning is the key to a successful expedition. Work in small groups to plan your expedition. When your group has finished planning, meet with your class to present your program. Consider these questions and issues in making your plan:

◆ What research will you do—weather, wildlife, geology, or another topic?

◆ Where will you work? Will you work near the coast? Will you join an existing research station?

◆ Will you travel? Plot your travel course and location on a map of Antarctica.

◆ How long do you plan to stay?

◆ What equipment will you take—climbing gear to cross glaciers, boats and kayaks, tents for camping?

◆ What clothing will you need? Check the illustration of protective clothing.

◆ What supplies will you take? Plan the kinds and amounts of food that you will take.

Think Like a Scientist

Although you may not know it, you think like a scientist every day. Whenever you ask a question and explore possible answers, you use many of the same skills that scientists do. Some of these skills are described on this page.

Observing

When you use one or more of your five senses to gather information about the world, you are **observing.** Hearing a dog bark, counting twelve green seeds, and smelling smoke are all observations. To increase the power of their senses, scientists sometimes use microscopes, telescopes, or other instruments that help them make more detailed observations.

An observation must be an accurate report of what your senses detect. It is important to keep careful records of your observations in science class by writing or drawing in a notebook. The information collected through observations is called evidence, or data.

Inferring

When you interpret an observation, you are **inferring,** or making an inference. For example, if you hear your dog barking, you may infer that someone is at your front door. To make this inference, you combine the evidence—the barking dog—and your experience or knowledge—you know that your dog barks when strangers approach—to reach a logical conclusion.

Notice that an inference is not a fact; it is only one of many possible interpretations for an observation. For example, your dog may be barking because it wants to go for a walk. An inference may turn out to be incorrect even if it is based on accurate observations and logical reasoning. The only way to find out if an inference is correct is to investigate further.

Predicting

When you listen to the weather forecast, you hear many predictions about the next day's weather—what the temperature will be, whether it will rain, and how windy it will be. Weather forecasters use observations and knowledge of weather patterns to predict the weather. The skill of **predicting** involves making an inference about a future event based on current evidence or past experience.

Because a prediction is an inference, it may prove to be false. In science class, you can test some of your predictions by doing experiments. For example, suppose you predict that larger paper airplanes can fly farther than smaller airplanes. How could you test your prediction?

ACTIVITY Use the photograph to answer the questions below.

Observing Look closely at the photograph. List at least three observations.

Inferring Use your observations to make an inference about what has happened. What experience or knowledge did you use to make the inference?

Predicting Predict what will happen next. On what evidence or experience do you base your prediction?

Classifying

Could you imagine searching for a book in the library if the books were shelved in no particular order? Your trip to the library would be an all-day event! Luckily, librarians group together books on similar topics or by the same author. Grouping together items that are alike in some way is called **classifying.** You can classify items in many ways: by size, by shape, by use, and by other important characteristics.

Like librarians, scientists use the skill of classifying to organize information and objects. When things are sorted into groups, the relationships among them become easier to understand.

Classify the objects in the photograph into two groups based on any characteristic you choose. Then use another characteristic to classify the objects into three groups.

ACTIVITY

Making Models

Have you ever drawn a picture to help someone understand what you were saying? Such a drawing is one type of model. A model is a picture, diagram, computer image, or other representation of a complex object or process. **Making models** helps people understand things that they cannot observe directly.

Scientists often use models to represent things that are either very large or very small, such as the planets in the solar system, or the parts of a cell. Such models are physical models—drawings or three-dimensional structures that look like the real thing. Other models are mental models—mathematical equations or words that describe how something works.

This student is using a model to demonstrate what causes day and night on Earth. What do the flashlight and the tennis ball in the model represent?

ACTIVITY

Communicating

Whenever you talk on the phone, write a letter, or listen to your teacher at school, you are communicating. **Communicating** is the process of sharing ideas and information with other people. Communicating effectively requires many skills, including writing, reading, speaking, listening, and making models.

Scientists communicate to share results, information, and opinions. Scientists often communicate about their work in journals, over the telephone, in letters, and on the Internet. They also attend scientific meetings where they share their ideas with one another in person.

On a sheet of paper, write out clear, detailed directions for tying your shoe. Then exchange directions with a partner. Follow your partner's directions exactly. How successful were you at tying your shoe? How could your partner have communicated more clearly?

ACTIVITY

Making Measurements

When scientists make observations, it is not sufficient to say that something is "big" or "heavy." Instead, scientists use instruments to measure just how big or heavy an object is. By measuring, scientists can express their observations more precisely and communicate more information about what they observe.

Measuring in SI

The standard system of measurement used by scientists around the world is known as the International System of Units, which is abbreviated as SI (in French, *Système International d'Unités*). SI units are easy to use because they are based on multiples of 10. Each unit is ten times larger than the next smallest unit and one tenth the size of the next largest unit. The table lists the prefixes used to name the most common SI units.

Common SI Prefixes

Prefix	Symbol	Meaning
kilo-	k	1,000
hecto-	h	100
deka-	da	10
deci-	d	0.1 (one tenth)
centi-	c	0.01 (one hundredth)
milli-	m	0.001 (one thousandth)

Length To measure length, or the distance between two points, the unit of measure is the **meter (m).** The distance from the floor to a doorknob is approximately one meter. Long distances, such as the distance between two cities, are measured in kilometers (km). Small lengths are measured in centimeters (cm) or millimeters (mm). Scientists use metric rulers and meter sticks to measure length.

Common Conversions

1 km = 1,000 m
1 m = 100 cm
1 m = 1,000 mm
1 cm = 10 mm

Liquid Volume To measure the volume of a liquid, or the amount of space it takes up, you will use a unit of measure known as the **liter (L).** One liter is the approximate volume of a medium-size carton of milk. Smaller volumes are measured in milliliters (mL). Scientists use graduated cylinders to measure liquid volume.

Common Conversion

1 L = 1,000 mL

ACTIVITY

The larger lines on the metric ruler in the picture show centimeter divisions, while the smaller, unnumbered lines show millimeter divisions. How many centimeters long is the shell? How many millimeters long is it?

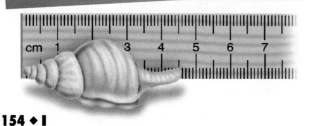

ACTIVITY

The graduated cylinder in the picture is marked in milliliter divisions. Notice that the water in the cylinder has a curved surface. This curved surface is called the *meniscus.* To measure the volume, you must read the level at the lowest point of the meniscus. What is the volume of water in this graduated cylinder?

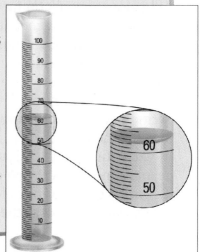

Mass To measure mass, or the amount of matter in an object, you will use a unit of measure known as the **gram (g)**. One gram is approximately the mass of a paper clip. Larger masses are measured in kilograms (kg). Scientists use a balance to find the mass of an object.

Common Conversion

1 kg = 1,000 g

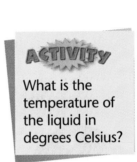

The mass of the apple in the picture is measured in kilograms. What is the mass of the apple? Suppose a recipe for applesauce called for one kilogram of apples. About how many apples would you need?

ACTIVITY

Temperature
To measure the temperature of a substance, you will use the **Celsius scale.** Temperature is measured in degrees Celsius (°C) using a Celsius thermometer. Water freezes at 0°C and boils at 100°C.

ACTIVITY

What is the temperature of the liquid in degrees Celsius?

Converting SI Units

To use the SI system, you must know how to convert between units. Converting from one unit to another involves the skill of **calculating**, or using mathematical operations. Converting between SI units is similar to converting between dollars and dimes because both systems are based on multiples of ten.

Suppose you want to convert a length of 80 centimeters to meters. Follow these steps to convert between units.

1. Begin by writing down the measurement you want to convert—in this example, 80 centimeters.
2. Write a conversion factor that represents the relationship between the two units you are converting. In this example, the relationship is *1 meter = 100 centimeters*. Write this conversion factor as a fraction, making sure to place the units you are converting from (centimeters, in this example) in the denominator.

3. Multiply the measurement you want to convert by the fraction. When you do this, the units in the first measurement will cancel out with the units in the denominator. Your answer will be in the units you are converting to (meters, in this example).

Example

80 centimeters = ___?___ meters

$$80 \text{ centimeters} \times \frac{1 \text{ meter}}{100 \text{ centimeters}} = \frac{80 \text{ meters}}{100}$$

$$= 0.8 \text{ meters}$$

Convert between the following units.

ACTIVITY

1. 600 millimeters = _?_ meters
2. 0.35 liters = _?_ milliliters
3. 1,050 grams = _?_ kilograms

Conducting a Scientific Investigation

In some ways, scientists are like detectives, piecing together clues to learn about a process or event. One way that scientists gather clues is by carrying out experiments. An experiment tests an idea in a careful, orderly manner. Although experiments do not all follow the same steps in the same order, many follow a pattern similar to the one described here.

Posing Questions

Experiments begin by asking a scientific question. A scientific question is one that can be answered by gathering evidence. For example, the question "Which freezes faster— fresh water or salt water?" is a scientific question because you can carry out an investigation and gather information to answer the question.

Developing a Hypothesis

The next step is to form a hypothesis. A **hypothesis** is a possible explanation for a set of observations or answer to a scientific question. In science, a hypothesis must be something that can be tested. A hypothesis can be worded as an *If...then...*statement. For example, a hypothesis might be *"If I add salt to fresh water, then the water will take longer to freeze."* A hypothesis worded this way serves as a rough outline of the experiment you should perform.

Designing an Experiment

Next you need to plan a way to test your hypothesis. Your plan should be written out as a step-by-step procedure and should describe the observations or measurements you will make.

Two important steps involved in designing an experiment are controlling variables and forming operational definitions.

Controlling Variables In a well-designed experiment, you need to keep all variables the same except for one. A **variable** is any factor that can change in an experiment. The factor that you change is called the **manipulated variable.** In this experiment, the manipulated variable is the amount of salt added to the water. Other factors, such as the amount of water or the starting temperature, are kept constant.

The factor that changes as a result of the manipulated variable is called the responding variable. The **responding variable** is what you measure or observe to obtain your results. In this experiment, the responding variable is how long the water takes to freeze.

An experiment in which all factors except one are kept constant is a **controlled experiment.** Most controlled experiments include a test called the control. In this experiment, Container 3 is the control. Because no salt is added to Container 3, you can compare the results from the other containers to it. Any difference in results must be due to the addition of salt alone.

Forming Operational Definitions
Another important aspect of a well-designed experiment is having clear operational definitions. An **operational definition** is a statement that describes how a particular variable is to be measured or how a term is to be defined. For example, in this experiment, how will you determine if the water has frozen? You might decide to insert a stick in each container at the start of the experiment. Your operational definition of "frozen" would be the time at which the stick can no longer move.

EXPERIMENTAL PROCEDURE

1. Fill 3 containers with 300 milliliters of cold tap water.

2. Add 10 grams of salt to Container 1; stir. Add 20 grams of salt to Container 2; stir. Add no salt to Container 3.

3. Place the 3 containers in a freezer.

4. Check the containers every 15 minutes. Record your observations.

Interpreting Data

The observations and measurements you make in an experiment are called data. At the end of an experiment, you need to analyze the data to look for any patterns or trends. Patterns often become clear if you organize your data in a data table or graph. Then think through what the data reveal. Do they support your hypothesis? Do they point out a flaw in your experiment? Do you need to collect more data?

Drawing Conclusions

A conclusion is a statement that sums up what you have learned from an experiment. When you draw a conclusion, you need to decide whether the data you collected support your hypothesis or not. You may need to repeat an experiment several times before you can draw any conclusions from it. Conclusions often lead you to pose new questions and plan new experiments to answer them.

Is a ball's bounce affected by the height from which it is dropped? Using the steps just described, plan a controlled experiment to investigate this problem.

ACTIVITY

Thinking Critically

Has a friend ever asked for your advice about a problem? If so, you may have helped your friend think through the problem in a logical way. Without knowing it, you used critical-thinking skills to help your friend. Critical thinking involves the use of reasoning and logic to solve problems or make decisions. Some critical-thinking skills are described below.

Comparing and Contrasting

When you examine two objects for similarities and differences, you are using the skill of **comparing and contrasting.** Comparing involves identifying similarities, or common characteristics. Contrasting involves identifying differences. Analyzing objects in this way can help you discover details that you might otherwise overlook.

ACTIVITY

Compare and contrast the two animals in the photo. First list all the similarities that you see. Then list all the differences.

Applying Concepts

When you use your knowledge about one situation to make sense of a similar situation, you are using the skill of **applying concepts.** Being able to transfer your knowledge from one situation to another shows that you truly understand a concept. You may use this skill in answering test questions that present different problems from the ones you've reviewed in class.

ACTIVITY

You have just learned that water takes longer to freeze when other substances are mixed into it. Use this knowledge to explain why people need a substance called antifreeze in their car's radiator in the winter.

Interpreting Illustrations

Diagrams, photographs, and maps are included in textbooks to help clarify what you read. These illustrations show processes, places, and ideas in a visual manner. The skillcalled **interpreting illustrations** canhelp you learn from these visual elements. To understand an illustration, take the time to study the illustration along with all the written information that accompanies it. Captions identify the key concepts shown in the illustration. Labels point out the important parts of a diagram or map, while keys identify the symbols used in a map.

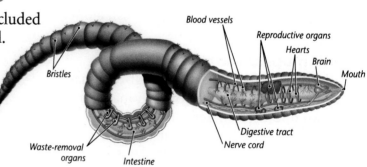

Blood vessels
Reproductive organs
Hearts
Brain
Mouth
Bristles
Digestive tract
Nerve cord
Waste-removal organs
Intestine

▲ **Internal anatomy of an earthworm**

ACTIVITY

Study the diagram above. Then write a short paragraph explaining what you have learned.

Relating Cause and Effect

If one event causes another event to occur, the two events are said to have a cause-and-effect relationship. When you determine that such a relationship exists between two events, you use a skill called **relating cause and effect.** For example, if you notice an itchy, red bump on your skin, you might infer that a mosquito bit you. The mosquito bite is the cause, and the bump is the effect.

It is important to note that two events do not necessarily have a cause-and-effect relationship just because they occur together. Scientists carry out experiments or use past experience to determine whether a cause-and-effect relationship exists.

ACTIVITY You are on a camping trip and your flashlight has stopped working. List some possible causes for the flashlight malfunction. How could you determine which cause-and-effect relationship has left you in the dark?

Making Generalizations

When you draw a conclusion about an entire group based on information about only some of the group's members, you are using a skill called **making generalizations.** For a generalization to be valid, the sample you choose must be large enough and representative of the entire group. You might, for example, put this skill to work at a farm stand if you see a sign that says, "Sample some grapes before you buy." If you sample a few sweet grapes, you may conclude that all the grapes are sweet—and purchase a large bunch.

ACTIVITY A team of scientists needs to determine whether the water in a large reservoir is safe to drink. How could they use the skill of making generalizations to help them? What should they do?

Making Judgments

When you evaluate something to decide whether it is good or bad, or right or wrong, you are using a skill called **making judgments.** For example, you make judgments when you decide to eat healthful foods or to pick up litter in a park. Before you make a judgment, you need to think through the pros and cons of a situation, and identify the values or standards that you hold.

ACTIVITY Should children and teens be required to wear helmets when bicycling? Explain why you feel the way you do.

Problem Solving

When you use critical-thinking skills to resolve an issue or decide on a course of action, you are using a skill called **problem solving.** Some problems, such as how to convert a fraction into a decimal, are straightforward. Other problems, such as figuring out why your computer has stopped working, are complex. Some complex problems can be solved using the trial and error method—try out one solution first, and if that doesn't work, try another. Other useful problem-solving strategies include making models and brainstorming possible solutions with a partner.

Organizing Information

As you read this textbook, how can you make sense of all the information it contains? Some useful tools to help you organize information are shown on this page. These tools are called *graphic organizers* because they give you a visual picture of a topic, showing at a glance how key concepts are related.

Concept Maps

Concept maps are useful tools for organizing information on broad topics. A concept map begins with a general concept and shows how it can be broken down into more specific concepts. In that way, relationships between concepts become easier to understand.

A concept map is constructed by placing concept words (usually nouns) in ovals and connecting them with linking words. Often, the most general concept word is placed at the top, and the words become more specific as you move downward. Often the linking words, which are written on a line extending between two ovals, describe the relationship between the two concepts they connect. If you follow any string of concepts and linking words down the map, it should read like a sentence.

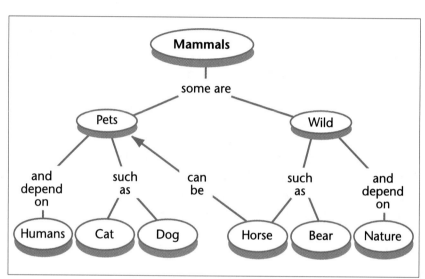

Some concept maps include linking words that connect a concept on one branch of the map to a concept on another branch. These linking words, called cross-linkages, show more complex interrelationships among concepts.

Compare/Contrast Tables

Compare/contrast tables are useful tools for sorting out the similarities and differences between two or more items. A table provides an organized framework in which to compare items based on specific characteristics that you identify.

To create a compare/contrast table, list the items to be compared across the top of a table. Then list the characteristics that will form the basis of your comparison in the left-hand

Characteristic	Baseball	Basketball
Number of Players	9	5
Playing Field	Baseball diamond	Basketball court
Equipment	Bat, baseball, mitts	Basket, basketball

column. Complete the table by filling in information about each characteristic, first for one item and then for the other.

Venn Diagrams

Another way to show similarities and differences between items is with a Venn diagram. A Venn diagram consists of two or more circles that partially overlap. Each circle represents a particular concept or idea. Common characteristics, or similarities, are written within the area of overlap between the two circles. Unique characteristics, or differences, are written in the parts of the circles outside the area of overlap.

To create a Venn diagram, draw two over-lapping circles. Label the circles with the names of the items being compared. Write the

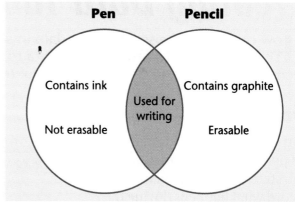

Pen   **Pencil**

Contains ink | Used for writing | Contains graphite
Not erasable | | Erasable

unique characteristics in each circle outside the area of overlap. Then write the shared characteristics within the area of overlap.

Flowcharts

A flowchart can help you understand the order in which certain events have occurred or should occur. Flowcharts are useful for outlining the stages in a process or the steps in a procedure.

To make a flowchart, write a brief description of each event in a box. Place the first event at the top of the page, followed by the second event, the third event, and so on. Then draw an arrow to connect each event to the one that occurs next.

Preparing Pasta

Boil water
↓
Cook pasta
↓
Drain water
↓
Add sauce

Cycle Diagrams

A cycle diagram can be used to show a sequence of events that is continuous, or cyclical. A continuous sequence does not have an end because, when the final event is over, the first event begins again. Like a flowchart, a cycle diagram can help you understand the order of events.

To create a cycle diagram, write a brief description of each event in a box. Place one event at the top of the page in the center. Then, moving in a clockwise direction around an imaginary circle, write each event in its proper sequence. Draw arrows that connect each event to the one that occurs next, forming a continuous circle.

Steps in a Science Experiment

Pose a question → Develop a hypothesis → Design an experiment → Interpret data → Draw conclusions → (Pose a question)

Creating Data Tables and Graphs

How can you make sense of the data in a science experiment? The first step is to organize the data to help you understand them. Data tables and graphs are helpful tools for organizing data.

Data Tables

You have gathered your materials and set up your experiment. But before you start, you need to plan a way to record what happens during the experiment. By creating a data table, you can record your observations and measurements in an orderly way.

Suppose, for example, that a scientist conducted an experiment to find out how many Calories people of different body masses burn while doing various activities. The data table shows the results.

Notice in this data table that the manipulated variable (body mass) is the heading of one column. The responding variable (for Experiment 1, the number of Calories burned while bicycling) is the heading of the next column. Additional columns were added for related experiments.

CALORIES BURNED IN 30 MINUTES OF ACTIVITY

Body Mass	Experiment 1 Bicycling	Experiment 2 Playing Basketball	Experiment 3 Watching Television
30 kg	60 Calories	120 Calories	21 Calories
40 kg	77 Calories	164 Calories	27 Calories
50 kg	95 Calories	206 Calories	33 Calories
60 kg	114 Calories	248 Calories	38 Calories

Bar Graphs

To compare how many Calories a person burns doing various activities, you could create a bar graph. A bar graph is used to display data in a number of separate, or distinct, categories. In this example, bicycling, playing basketball, and watching television are three separate categories.

To create a bar graph, follow these steps.

1. On graph paper, draw a horizontal, or *x*-, axis and a vertical, or *y*-, axis.
2. Write the names of the categories to be graphed along the horizontal axis. Include an overall label for the axis as well.
3. Label the vertical axis with the name of the responding variable. Include units of measurement. Then create a scale along the axis by marking off equally spaced numbers that cover the range of the data collected.
4. For each category, draw a solid bar using the scale on the vertical axis to determine the

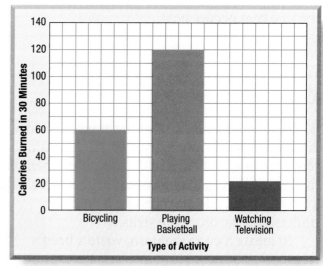

Calories Burned by a 30-kilogram Person in Various Activities

appropriate height. For example, for bicycling, draw the bar as high as the 60 mark on the vertical axis. Make all the bars the same width and leave equal spaces between them.
5. Add a title that describes the graph.

Line Graphs

To see whether a relationship exists between body mass and the number of Calories burned while bicycling, you could create a line graph. A line graph is used to display data that show how one variable (the responding variable) changes in response to another variable (the manipulated variable). You can use a line graph when your manipulated variable is *continuous,* that is, when there are other points between the ones that you tested. In this example, body mass is a continuous variable because there are other body masses between 30 and 40 kilograms (for example, 31 kilograms). Time is another example of a continuous variable.

   Line graphs are powerful tools because they allow you to estimate values for conditions that you did not test in the experiment. For example, you can use the line graph to estimate that a 35-kilogram person would burn 68 Calories while bicycling.

To create a line graph, follow these steps.
1. On graph paper, draw a horizontal, or *x-,* axis and a vertical, or *y-,* axis.
2. Label the horizontal axis with the name of the manipulated variable. Label the vertical axis with the name of the responding variable. Include units of measurement.
3. Create a scale on each axis by marking off equally spaced numbers that cover the range of the data collected.
4. Plot a point on the graph for each piece of data. In the line graph above, the dotted lines show how to plot the first data point (30 kilograms and 60 Calories). Draw an imaginary vertical line extending up from the horizontal axis at the 30-kilogram mark. Then draw an imaginary horizontal line extending across from the vertical axis at the 60-Calorie mark. Plot the point where the two lines intersect.

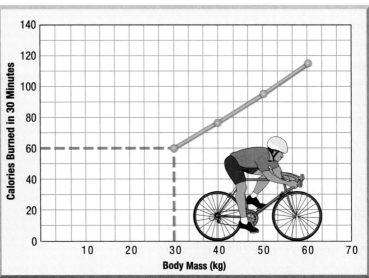

Effect of Body Mass on Calories Burned While Bicycling

5. Connect the plotted points with a solid line. (In some cases, it may be more appropriate to draw a line that shows the general trend of the plotted points. In those cases, some of the points may fall above or below the line. Also, not all graphs are linear. It may be more appropriate to draw a curve to connect the points.)
6. Add a title that identifies the variables or relationship in the graph.

Create line graphs to display the data from Experiment 2 and Experiment 3 in the data table. **ACTIVITY**

You read in the newspaper that a total of 4 centimeters of rain fell in your area in June, 2.5 centimeters fell in July, and 1.5 centimeters fell in August. What type of graph would you use to display these data? Use graph paper to create the graph. **ACTIVITY**

Circle Graphs

Like bar graphs, circle graphs can be used to display data in a number of separate categories. Unlike bar graphs, however, circle graphs can only be used when you have data for *all* the categories that make up a given topic. A circle graph is sometimes called a pie chart because it resembles a pie cut into slices. The pie represents the entire topic, while the slices represent the individual categories. The size of a slice indicates what percentage of the whole a particular category makes up.

   The data table below shows the results of a survey in which 24 teenagers were asked to identify their favorite sport. The data were then used to create the circle graph at the right.

Sports That Teens Prefer

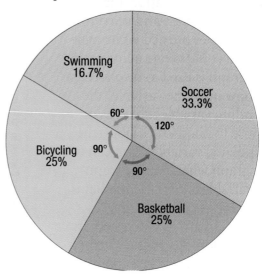

FAVORITE SPORTS

Sport	Number of Students
Soccer	8
Basketball	6
Bicycling	6
Swimming	4

To create a circle graph, follow these steps.
1. Use a compass to draw a circle. Mark the center of the circle with a point. Then draw a line from the center point to the top of the circle.
2. Determine the size of each "slice" by setting up a proportion where x equals the number of degrees in a slice. (NOTE: A circle contains 360 degrees.) For example, to find the number of degrees in the "soccer" slice, set up the following proportion:

$$\frac{\text{students who prefer soccer}}{\text{total number of students}} = \frac{x}{\text{total number of degrees in a circle}}$$

$$\frac{8}{24} = \frac{x}{360}$$

Cross-multiply and solve for x.

$$24x = 8 \times 360$$
$$x = 120$$

The "soccer" slice should contain 120 degrees.

3. Use a protractor to measure the angle of the first slice, using the line you drew to the top of the circle as the 0° line. Draw a line from the center of the circle to the edge for the angle you measured.
4. Continue around the circle by measuring the size of each slice with the protractor. Start measuring from the edge of the previous slice so the wedges do not overlap. When you are done, the entire circle should be filled in.
5. Determine the percentage of the whole circle that each slice represents. To do this, divide the number of degrees in a slice by the total number of degrees in a circle (360), and multiply by 100%. For the "soccer" slice, you can find the percentage as follows:

$$\frac{120}{360} \times 100\% = 33.3\%$$

6. Use a different color to shade in each slice. Label each slice with the name of the category and with the percentage of the whole it represents.
7. Add a title to the circle graph.

ACTIVITY

In a class of 28 students, 12 students take the bus to school, 10 students walk, and 6 students ride their bicycles. Create a circle graph to display these data.

Laboratory Safety

Safety Symbols

These symbols alert you to possible dangers in the laboratory and remind you to work carefully.

Safety Goggles Always wear safety goggles to protect your eyes in any activity involving chemicals, flames or heating, or the possibility of broken glassware.

Lab Apron Wear a laboratory apron to protect your skin and clothing from damage.

Breakage You are working with materials that may be breakable, such as glass containers, glass tubing, thermometers, or funnels. Handle breakable materials with care. Do not touch broken glassware.

Heat-resistant Gloves Use an oven mitt or other hand protection when handling hot materials. Hot plates, hot glassware, or hot water can cause burns. Do not touch hot objects with your bare hands.

Heating Use a clamp or tongs to pick up hot glassware. Do not touch hot objects with your bare hands.

Sharp Object Pointed-tip scissors, scalpels, knives, needles, pins, or tacks are sharp. They can cut or puncture your skin. Always direct a sharp edge or point away from yourself and others. Use sharp instruments only as instructed.

Electric Shock Avoid the possibility of electric shock. Never use electrical equipment around water, or when the equipment is wet or your hands are wet. Be sure cords are untangled and cannot trip anyone. Disconnect the equipment when it is not in use.

Corrosive Chemical You are working with an acid or another corrosive chemical. Avoid getting it on your skin or clothing, or in your eyes. Do not inhale the vapors. Wash your hands when you are finished with the activity.

Poison Do not let any poisonous chemical come in contact with your skin, and do not inhale its vapors. Wash your hands when you are finished with the activity.

Physical Safety When an experiment involves physical activity, take precautions to avoid injuring yourself or others. Follow instructions from your teacher. Alert your teacher if there is any reason you should not participate in the activity.

Animal Safety Treat live animals with care to avoid harming the animals or yourself. Working with animal parts or preserved animals also may require caution. Wash your hands when you are finished with the activity.

Plant Safety Handle plants in the laboratory or during field work only as directed by your teacher. If you are allergic to certain plants, tell your teacher before doing an activity in which those plants are used. Avoid touching harmful plants such as poison ivy, poison oak, or poison sumac, or plants with thorns. Wash your hands when you are finished with the activity.

Flames You may be working with flames from a lab burner, candle, or matches. Tie back loose hair and clothing. Follow instructions from your teacher about lighting and extinguishing flames.

No Flames Flammable materials may be present. Make sure there are no flames, sparks, or other exposed heat sources present.

Fumes When poisonous or unpleasant vapors may be involved, work in a ventilated area. Avoid inhaling vapors directly. Only test an odor when directed to do so by your teacher, and use a wafting motion to direct the vapor toward your nose.

Disposal Chemicals and other laboratory materials used in the activity must be disposed of safely. Follow the instructions from your teacher.

Hand Washing Wash your hands thoroughly when finished with the activity. Use antibacterial soap and warm water. Lather both sides of your hands and between your fingers. Rinse well.

General Safety Awareness You may see this symbol when none of the symbols described earlier appears. In this case, follow the specific instructions provided. You may also see this symbol when you are asked to develop your own procedure in a lab. Have your teacher approve your plan before you go further.

Science Safety Rules

To prepare yourself to work safely in the laboratory, read over the following safety rules. Then read them a second time. Make sure you understand and follow each rule. Ask your teacher to explain any rules you do not understand.

Dress Code

1. To protect yourself from injuring your eyes, wear safety goggles whenever you work with chemicals, burners, glassware, or any substance that might get into your eyes. If you wear contact lenses, notify your teacher.
2. Wear a lab apron or coat whenever you work with corrosive chemicals or substances that can stain.
3. Tie back long hair to keep it away from any chemicals, flames, or equipment.
4. Remove or tie back any article of clothing or jewelry that can hang down and touch chemicals, flames, or equipment. Roll up or secure long sleeves.
5. Never wear open shoes or sandals.

General Precautions

6. Read all directions for an experiment several times before beginning the activity. Carefully follow all written and oral instructions. If you are in doubt about any part of the experiment, ask your teacher for assistance.
7. Never perform activities that are not assigned or authorized by your teacher. Obtain permission before "experimenting" on your own. Never handle any equipment unless you have specific permission.
8. Never perform lab activities without direct supervision.
9. Never eat or drink in the laboratory.
10. Keep work areas clean and tidy at all times. Bring only notebooks and lab manuals or written lab procedures to the work area. All other items, such as purses and backpacks, should be left in a designated area.
11. Do not engage in horseplay.

First Aid

12. Always report all accidents or injuries to your teacher, no matter how minor. Notify your teacher immediately about any fires.
13. Learn what to do in case of specific accidents, such as getting acid in your eyes or on your skin. (Rinse acids from your body with lots of water.)
14. Be aware of the location of the first-aid kit, but do not use it unless instructed by your teacher. In case of injury, your teacher should administer first aid. Your teacher may also send you to the school nurse or call a physician.
15. Know the location of emergency equipment, such as the fire extinguisher and fire blanket, and know how to use it.
16. Know the location of the nearest telephone and whom to contact in an emergency.

Heating and Fire Safety

17. Never use a heat source, such as a candle, burner, or hot plate, without wearing safety goggles.
18. Never heat anything unless instructed to do so. A chemical that is harmless when cool may be dangerous when heated.
19. Keep all combustible materials away from flames. Never use a flame or spark near a combustible chemical.
20. Never reach across a flame.
21. Before using a laboratory burner, make sure you know proper procedures for lighting and adjusting the burner, as demonstrated by your teacher. Do not touch the burner. It may be hot. And never leave a lighted burner unattended!
22. Chemicals can splash or boil out of a heated test tube. When heating a substance in a test tube, make sure that the mouth of the tube is not pointed at you or anyone else.
23. Never heat a liquid in a closed container. The expanding gases produced may blow the container apart.
24. Before picking up a container that has been heated, hold the back of your hand near it. If you can feel heat on the back of your hand, the container is too hot to handle. Use an oven mitt to pick up a container that has been heated.

Using Chemicals Safely

25. Never mix chemicals "for the fun of it." You might produce a dangerous, possibly explosive substance.

26. Never put your face near the mouth of a container that holds chemicals. Many chemicals are poisonous. Never touch, taste, or smell a chemical unless you are instructed by your teacher to do so.

27. Use only those chemicals needed in the activity. Read and double-check labels on supply bottles before removing any chemicals. Take only as much as you need. Keep all containers closed when chemicals are not being used.

28. Dispose of all chemicals as instructed by your teacher. To avoid contamination, never return chemicals to their original containers. Never simply pour chemicals or other substances into the sink or trash containers.

29. Be extra careful when working with acids or bases. Pour all chemicals over the sink or a container, not over your work surface.

30. If you are instructed to test for odors, use a wafting motion to direct the odors to your nose. Do not inhale the fumes directly from the container.

31. When mixing an acid and water, always pour the water into the container first and then add the acid to the water. Never pour water into an acid.

32. Take extreme care not to spill any material in the laboratory. Wash chemical spills and splashes immediately with plenty of water. Immediately begin rinsing with water any acids that get on your skin or clothing, and notify your teacher of any acid spill at the same time.

Using Glassware Safely

33. Never force glass tubing or thermometers into a rubber stopper or rubber tubing. Have your teacher insert the glass tubing or thermometer if required for an activity.

34. If you are using a laboratory burner, use a wire screen to protect glassware from any flame. Never heat glassware that is not thoroughly dry on the outside.

35. Keep in mind that hot glassware looks cool. Never pick up glassware without first checking to see if it is hot. Use an oven mitt. See rule 24.

36. Never use broken or chipped glassware. If glassware breaks, notify your teacher and dispose of the glassware in the proper broken-glassware container. Never handle broken glass with your bare hands.

37. Never eat or drink from lab glassware.

38. Thoroughly clean glassware before putting it away.

Using Sharp Instruments

39. Handle scalpels or other sharp instruments with extreme care. Never cut material toward you; cut away from you.

40. Immediately notify your teacher if you cut your skin when working in the laboratory.

Animal and Plant Safety

41. Never perform experiments that cause pain, discomfort, or harm to animals. This rule applies at home as well as in the classroom.

42. Animals should be handled only if absolutely necessary. Your teacher will instruct you as to how to handle each animal species brought into the classroom.

43. If you know that you are allergic to certain plants, molds, or animals, tell your teacher before doing an activity in which these are used.

44. During field work, protect your skin by wearing long pants, long sleeves, socks, and closed shoes. Know how to recognize the poisonous plants and fungi in your area, as well as plants with thorns, and avoid contact with them. Never eat any part of a plant or fungus.

45. Wash your hands thoroughly after handling animals or a cage containing animals. Wash your hands when you are finished with any activity involving animal parts, plants, or soil.

End-of-Experiment Rules

46. After an experiment has been completed, turn off all burners or hot plates. If you used a gas burner, check that the gas-line valve to the burner is off. Unplug hot plates.

47. Turn off and unplug any other electrical equipment that you used.

48. Clean up your work area and return all equipment to its proper place.

49. Dispose of waste materials as instructed by your teacher.

50. Wash your hands after every experiment.

Glossary

acid rain Rain that contains more acid than normal. (p. 23)

air mass A huge body of air that has similar temperature, pressure, and humidity throughout. (p. 76)

air pressure A force that is the result of the weight of a column of air pushing down on an area. (p. 26)

altitude Elevation above sea level. (p. 28)

anemometer An instrument used to measure wind speed. (p. 53)

aneroid barometer An instrument that measures changes in air pressure without using a liquid. Changes in the shape of an airtight metal box cause a needle on the barometer dial to move. (p. 27)

anticyclone A high-pressure center of dry air. (p. 82)

atmosphere The layer of gases that surrounds Earth. (p. 14)

aurora borealis A colorful, glowing display in the sky caused when particles from the sun strike oxygen and nitrogen atoms in the ionosphere; also called the Northern Lights. (p. 36)

.... **B** ....

barometer An instrument used to measure changes in air pressure. (p. 26)

.... **C** ....

chlorofluorocarbons Chlorine compounds formerly used in air conditioners, refrigerators, and spray cans; also called CFCs. (p. 142)

cirrus Wispy, feathery clouds made mostly of ice crystals that form at high levels, above about 6 kilometers. (p. 64)

climate The average, year-after-year conditions of temperature, precipitation, winds, and clouds in an area. (p. 112)

condensation The process by which molecules of water vapor in the air become liquid water. (p. 63)

conduction The direct transfer of heat from one substance to another substance that it is touching. (p. 50)

continental (air mass) A dry air mass that forms over land. (p. 76)

continental climate The climate of the centers of continents, with cold winters and warm or hot summers. (p. 114)

controlled experiment An experiment in which all factors except one are kept constant. (p. 153)

convection The transfer of heat by the movement of a fluid. (p. 50)

Coriolis effect The way Earth's rotation makes winds in the Northern Hemisphere curve to the right and winds in the Southern Hemisphere curve to the left. (p. 57)

cumulus Clouds that form less than 2 kilometers above the ground and look like fluffy, rounded piles of cotton. (p. 64)

cyclone A swirling center of low air pressure. (p. 81)

.... **D** ....

density The amount of mass of a substance to a given volume. (p. 25)

desert A region that gets less than 25 centimeters of rain a year. (p. 126)

dew point The temperature at which condensation begins. (p. 63)

droughts Long periods of low precipitation. (p. 70)

.... **E** ....

El Niño An event that occurs every two to seven years in the Pacific Ocean, during which winds shift and push warm surface water toward the coast of South America; it can cause dramatic climate changes. (p. 104)

electromagnetic wave A form of energy that can travel through space. (p. 42)

evacuate To move away temporarily. (p. 90)

evaporation The process by which water molecules in liquid water escape into the air as water vapor. (p. 61)

exosphere The outer layer of the thermosphere, extending outward into space. (p. 36)

.... **F** ....

flash flood A sudden, violent flood that occurs within a few hours, or even minutes, of a heavy rainstorm. (p. 96)

front The area where air masses meet and do not mix. (p. 79)

.... **G** ....

global warming A gradual increase in the temperature of Earth's atmosphere. (p. 140)

global winds Winds that blow steadily from specific directions over long distances. (p. 57)

greenhouse effect The process by which heat is trapped in the atmosphere by water vapor, carbon dioxide, methane, and other gases that form a "blanket" around Earth. (p. 45)

greenhouse gases Gases in the atmosphere that trap heat. (p. 140)

.... **H** ....

heat The energy transferred from a hotter object to a cooler one. (p. 49)

humid subtropical A wet and warm climate area on the edge of the tropics. (p. 128)

humidity A measure of the amount of water vapor in the air. (p. 62)

hurricane A tropical storm that has winds of 119 kilometers per hour or higher; typically about 600 kilometers across. (p. 88)

hypothesis A possible explanation for a set of observations or answer to a scientific question; must be testable. (p. 152)

ice ages Cold time periods in Earth's history, during which glaciers covered large parts of the surface. (p. 136)

infrared radiation A form of energy with wavelengths that are longer than visible light. (p. 43)

ionosphere The lower part of the thermosphere, where electrically charged particles called ions are found. (p. 36)

isobars Lines on a map joining places that have the same air pressure. (p. 104)

isotherms Lines on a map joining places that have the same temperature. (p. 104)

jet streams Bands of high-speed winds about 10 kilometers above Earth's surface. (p. 60)

land breeze The flow of air from land to a body of water. (p. 56)

latitude The distance from the equator, measured in degrees. (p. 58)

leeward The downwind side of mountains. (p. 117)

lightning A sudden spark, or energy discharge, caused when electrical charges jump between parts of a cloud or between a cloud and the ground. (p. 84)

local winds Winds that blow over short distances. (p. 54)

manipulated variable The one factor that a scientist changes during an experiment. (p. 153)

marine climate The climate of some coastal regions, with relatively warm winters and cool summers. (p. 114)

maritime (air mass) A humid air mass that forms over oceans. (p. 76)

mercury barometer An instrument that measures changes in air pressure, consisting of a glass tube partially filled with mercury, with its open end resting in a dish of mercury. Air pressure pushing on the mercury in the dish forces the mercury in the tube higher. (p. 26)

mesosphere The middle layer of Earth's atmosphere; the layer in which most meteoroids burn up. (p. 32)

meteorologists Scientists who study the causes of weather and try to predict it. (p. 102)

microclimate The climate characteristic of a small, specific area; it may be different from the climate of the surrounding area. (p. 117)

monsoons Sea and land breezes over a large region that change direction with the seasons. (p. 56)

occluded Cut off, as the warm air mass at an occluded front is cut off from the ground by cooler air beneath it. (p. 81)

operational definition A statement that describes how a particular variable is to be measured or a term is to be defined. (p. 153)

ozone A form of oxygen that has three oxygen atoms in each molecule instead of the usual two. (p. 16)

permafrost Permanently frozen soil found in the tundra climate region. (p. 130)

photochemical smog A brownish haze that is a mixture of ozone and other chemicals formed when nitrogen oxides, hydrocarbons, and other pollutants react with each other in the presence of sunlight. (p. 22)

polar (air mass) A cold air mass that forms north of 50° north latitude or south of 50° south latitude and has high air pressure. (p. 76)

polar zones The areas near both poles, from about 66.5° to 90° north and 66.5° to 90° south latitudes. (p. 113)

pollutants Harmful substances in the air, water, or soil. (p. 20)

precipitation Any form of water that falls from clouds and reaches Earth's surface. (p. 67)

pressure The force pushing on an area or surface. (p. 25)

psychrometer An instrument used to measure relative humidity, consisting of a wet-bulb thermometer and a dry-bulb thermometer. (p. 62)

radiation The direct transfer of energy by electromagnetic waves. (p. 42)

rain forest A forest in the tropical wet climate zone that gets plenty of rain all year. (p. 123)

rain gauge An instrument used to measure the amount of precipitation, consisting of an open-ended can topped by a collecting funnel and having a collecting tube and measuring scale inside. (p. 69)

relative humidity The percentage of water vapor in the air compared to the maximum amount the air could hold at that temperature. (p. 62)

responding variable The factor that changes as a result of changes to the manipulated variable in an experiment. (p. 153)

savanna A tropical grassland with scattered clumps of trees; found in the tropical wet-and-dry climate zone. (p. 126)

scattering Reflection of light in all directions. (p. 44)

sea breeze The flow of air from an ocean or lake to the land. (p. 56)

steppe A prairie or grassland found in the semiarid climate region. (p. 127)

storm A violent disturbance in the atmosphere. (p. 83)

storm surge A dome of water that sweeps across the coast where a hurricane lands. (p. 90)

stratosphere The second-lowest layer of Earth's atmosphere; the ozone layer is located in the upper stratosphere. (p. 32)

stratus Clouds that form in flat layers. (p. 64)

subarctic A climate zone that lies north of the humid continental climate zone, with short, cool summers and long, bitterly cold winters. (p. 129)

sunspots Dark, cooler regions on the surface of the sun. (p. 137)

temperate zones The area between the tropical and polar zones, from about 23.5° to 66.5° north and 23.5° to 66.5° south latitudes. (p. 113)

temperature The average amount of energy of motion in the molecules of a substance. (p. 49)

thermal energy The energy of motion in the molecules of a substance. (p. 49)

thermometer An instrument used to measure temperature, consisting of a thin, glass tube with a bulb on one end that contains a liquid (usually mercury or alcohol). (p. 49)

thermosphere The outermost layer of Earth's atmosphere. (p. 35)

tornado A rapidly whirling, funnel-shaped cloud that reaches down from a storm cloud to touch Earth's surface, usually leaving a destructive path. (p. 85)

tropical (air mass) A warm air mass that forms in the tropics and has low air pressure. (p. 76)

tropical zone The area near the equator, between about 23.5° north latitude and 23.5° south latitude. (p. 113)

troposphere The lowest layer of Earth's atmosphere, where weather occurs. (p. 31)

tundra A polar climate region, found across northern Alaska, Canada, and Russia, with short, cool summers and bitterly cold winters. (p. 130)

ultraviolet radiation A form of energy with wavelengths that are shorter than visible light. (p. 43)

variable Any factor that can change in an experiment. (p. 153)

water vapor Water in the form of a gas. (p. 17)

weather The condition of Earth's atmosphere at a particular time and place. (p. 14)

wind The horizontal movement of air from an area of high pressure to an area of lower pressure. (p. 52)

wind-chill factor Increased cooling caused by the wind. (p. 53)

windward The side of mountains that faces the oncoming wind. (p. 117)

Index

Acknowledgments

Staff Credits

The people who made up the **Science Explorer** team—representing design services, editorial, editorial services, electronic publishing technology, manufacturing & inventory planning, marketing, marketing services, market research, online services & multimedia development, production services, product planning, project office, and publishing processes—are listed below.

Carolyn Belanger, Barbara A. Bertell, Suzanne Biron, Peggy Bliss, Peter W. Brooks, Christopher R. Brown, Greg Cantone, Jonathan Cheney, Todd Christy, Lisa J. Clark, Patrick Finbarr Connolly, Edward Cordero, Robert Craton, Patricia Cully, Patricia M. Dambry, Kathleen J. Dempsey, Judy Elgin, Gayle Connolly Fedele, Frederick Fellows, Barbara Foster, Paula Foye, Loree Franz, Donald P. Gagnon Jr., Paul J. Gagnon, Joel Gendler, Elizabeth Good, Robert M. Graham, Kerri Hoar, Joanne Hudson, Linda D. Johnson, Anne Jones, Toby Klang, Carolyn Langley, Russ Lappa, Carolyn Lock, Cheryl Mahan, Dotti Marshall, Meredith Mascola, Jeanne Y. Maurand, Karen McHugh, Eve Melnechuk, Natania Mlawer, Paul W. Murphy, Cindy A. Noftle, Julia F. Osborne, Judi Pinkham, Caroline M. Power, Robin L. Santel, Suzanne J. Schineller, Emily Soltanoff, Kira Thaler-Marbit, Mark Tricca, Diane Walsh, Pearl Weinstein, Merce Wilczek, Helen Young.

Illustration

John Edwards & Associates: 30, 44, 56t, 79, 80, 81, 89, 119, 140
GeoSystems Global Corporation: 88, 91, 92, 103t, 115, 124–125, 136, 148
Andrea Golden: 10, 151
Jared Lee: 150
Martucci Design: 15, 23, 43, 103b, 121, 132
Matt Mayerchak: 37, 143
Morgan Cain & Associates: 26b, 27, 28, 39, 45, 48, 50–51, 54, 57, 59, 67, 69, 73, 141
Ortelius Design Inc: 17, 56b, 82, 86-87, 109, 113, 116, 138, 145
Matthew Pippin: 26t, 33, 61, 65, 96
Proof Positive/Farrowlyne Associates, Inc.: 149
John Sanderson/Horizon Design: 78
Walter Stuart: 137
J/B Woolsey Associates: 64, 97, 117, 145

Photography

Photo Research Kerri Hoar, PoYee McKenna Oster
Cover Image Tom Ives/The Stock Market

Nature of Science
Page 8, Jane Love/NASA; **9r,** Jose L. Pelaez/The Stock Market; **9l,** NASA/Photo Researchers; **10b,** NASA; **10–11t,** NASA

Chapter 1
Pages 12–13, Jay Simon/TSI; **14t,** Russ Lappa; **14b,** NASA/Photo Researchers; **16b,** Russ Lappa; **16t,** Richard Haynes; **17r,** George G. Dimijian/Photo Researchers; **18tl,** Eric Horan/Liaison International; **19,** Richard Haynes; **20t,** Russ Lappa; **20b,** Aaron Haupt/Photo Researchers; **21b,** Paul Lowe/Magnum Photos; **21t,** Biophoto Associates/Photo Researchers; **22,** Will McIntyre/Photo Researchers; **24,** Steve Casimiro/Liaison International; **25t,** Russ Lappa; **25b,** Eric A. Kessler; **27t,** Ivan Bucher/Photo Researchers; **29,** Russ Lappa; **31t,** Russ Lappa; **31b,** Steve Vidler/Superstock; **32,** Mark C. Burnett/Photo Researchers; **34b,** Corbis-Bettmann; **34t,** The Granger Collection, NY; **35b,** NASA; **35t,** The National Archives/Corbis; **36,** Jack Finch/Science Photo Library/Photo Researchers.

Chapter 2
Pages 40–41, William Johnson/Stock Boston; **42–43,** Photo Researchers; **47,** Richard Haynes; **48,** Russ Lappa; **49,** Russ Lappa; **50–51,** Daniel Cox/Allstock/PNI; **52t,** Russ Lappa; **52bl,** Victoria Hurst/Tom Stack & Associates; **52–53,** Gary Retherford/Photo Researchers; **53r,** Richard Haynes; **55,** Richard Haynes; **56,** Steve McCurry/Magnum Photos; **58,** Scala/Art Resource, NY; **60,** Ken McVey/TSI; **61,** Russ Lappa; **62,** E.J. Tarbuck; **63,** Peter Arnold; **65t,** Michael Gadomski/GADOM/Bruce Coleman; **65tm,** Phil Degginger/Bruce Coleman; **65bm,** E.R. Degginger; **65b,** John Shaw/Bruce Coleman; **66,** Wendy Shattil/Bob Rozinski/Tom Stack & Associates; **67,** Richard Haynes; **68t,** AP/Wide World; **68b,** Nuridsany et Perennou/Photo Researchers; **68 inset,** Gerben Oppermans/TSI; **70,** Bill Frantz/TSI; **71,** Victoria Hurst/Tom Stack & Associates.

Chapter 3
Pages 74–75, Pete Turner/The Image Bank; **76t,** Russ Lappa; **76b,** Russ Lappa; **77,** Jim Corwin/TSI; **83t,** Russ Lappa; **83b,** Dirck Halstead/Liaison International; **84,** Dan Sudia/Photo Researchers; **85,** Schuster/Superstock; **86b,** The Granger Collection, NY; **86t,** The Granger Collection, NY; **87l,** North Wind Picture Archives; **88,** Sheila Beougher/Liaison International; **89,** NASA-Goddard Laboratory for Atmospheres; **90,** Clore Collection, Tate Gallery, London/Art Resource, NY; **92,** NOAA; **94,** Tony Freeman/Photo Edit; **95t,** Richard Haynes; **95bl,** Keith Kent/Science Photo Library/Photo Researchers; **95br,** Grant V. Faint/The Image Bank; **98,** AP Photo/Pool/David J. Phillip; **99t,** Larry Lawfer; **99b,** Corel Corp.; **100,** AP Photo/David Umberger; **101,** NOAA; **103,** NOAA; **104–106,** AccuWeather, Inc.; **107,** Schuster/Superstock;.

Chapter 4
Pages 110–111, David Muench; **112t,** Richard Haynes; **112b,** Thomas D. Mangelsen/Peter Arnold; **114,** David Madison/Bruce Coleman; **116,** Duncan Wherrett/TSI; **117,** Chris Cheadle/TSI; **121,** Richard Haynes; **122t,** Russ Lappa; **122b,** Charlie Waite/TSI; **123,** Geogory G. Dimigian/Photo Researchers; **126t,** Thomas D. Mangelsen/Peter Arnold; **126b,** Alex S. MacLean/Peter Arnold; **127,** Stephen Johnson/TSI; **128t,** Ann Duncan/Tom Stack & Associates; **128b,** Margaret Gowan/TSI; **129,** Kennan Ward Photography/Corbis; **130t,** Art Wolfe/TSI; **130b,** Thomas Kitchin/Tom Stack & Associates; **131,** Photodisc, Inc.; **134,** 1996 Ira Block; **135r,** Tony Craddock/Science Photo Library/Photo Researchers; **135 inset,** George Godfrey/Animals Animals; **142,** NOAA; **143,** Tony Craddock/Science Photo Library/Photo Researchers.

Interdisciplinary Exploration
Page 146, Galen Rowell/Corbis; **147,** The Granger Collection, NY; **149,** AE Zuckerman/Photo Edit; **150 inset,** Corbis-Bettmann; **150–151,** AE Zuckerman/Photo Edit.

Skills Handbook
Page 152, Mike Moreland/Photo Network; **153t,** Foodpix; **153m,** Richard Haynes; **153b,** Russ Lappa; **156,** Richard Haynes; **158,** Ron Kimball; **159,** Renee Lynn/Photo Researchers.